Planning for Wi

MW01133671

JAMES SCHWAB, AICP, AND STUART MECK, FAICP, WITH JAMIE SIMONE

TABLE OF CONTENTS

Acknowledgments

This report was underwritten by the National Wildland/Urban Interface Fire Program, a cooperative interagency program operated by the National Fire Protection Association (NFPA), with headquarters in Quincy, Massachusetts. The authors wish to acknowledge the assistance and advice of Michele Steinberg, Firewise Communities Support Manager, and James Smalley, Manager, Wildland Fire Protection, for NFPA, as well as Ron Montague, vice president of Firewise 2000, Inc., a frequent consultant to the national program. In addition, the authors wish to thank the following for their insights in reviewing the draft manuscript: Nan Johnson, planner and Communities/Counties Coordinator with the Colorado State Forest Service; Hank Blackwell, Fire Marshal for Santa Fe County, New Mexico; Sue E. Pratt, AICP, principal planner for Coconino County Community Development, in Arizona; and Kenneth C. Topping, FAICP, principal of Topping Associates International, in Cambria, California. Michele Steinberg and Ron Montague also provided review comments. We would also like to thank all those, listed in Appendix B, who generously shared their time to provide insights as part of the survey of experts for this project. Finally, we wish to thank the following for their assistance in supplying illustrations: Jeff Bielling, Florida Department of Community Affairs; Lincoln Walther, Continental Shelf Associates; James Smalley, NFPA; and Ron Montague.

CHAPTER 1

Wildfires as a Planning Priority

n recent years, wildfires have routinely grabbed public attention through dramatic news stories. Wildfires are among the most photogenic of disasters, but that is not the only reason to pay attention. They are rapidly emerging as a serious question for land-use planning. As development spreads into high-risk fire zones, wildfires destroy homes, take lives, degrade air quality, burn hazardous materials that would not otherwise be present, and produce serious ecological damage. In addition, they often help effectuate subsequent disasters, such as landslides when rains sweep soil down hills denuded of vegetation. Those disasters, by producing even more dead and dying vegetation, can spawn more powerful wildfires unless measures are taken to remove the debris. Doing so is neither a cheap task nor a small one: Following massive wildfires in Southern California in October 2003, a storm on Christmas Day in San Bernardino County resulted in a flood that killed 16 people. Subsequently, contractors hauled away more than 50,000 truckloads of debris at a cost to federal taxpayers of $9 million (Watson and McCarthy 2004).

Still, one factor stands out above all others—more people are choosing to live in fire-prone wildlands than ever before, yet many, perhaps most, are only minimally aware of the requirements for successful coexistence with nature in such a hazardous context. Often they have little understanding of the level of risk they have assumed or how to mitigate it effectively. Moreover, there is often not enough debate within the larger community about the wisdom of permitting such development in the first place and under what circumstances it would be acceptable.

The problem is not isolated but national in scope. Just since 2000, several devastating wildfires have occurred:

- In Los Alamos, New Mexico, the Cerro Grande fire in May 2000 burned 47,650 acres and destroyed 235 structures while also damaging the Los Alamos National Laboratory. This wildfire was unusual in that it began as a prescribed burn, a mitigation technique, but soon spread beyond control.

- In Colorado's Front Range, the Hayman fire in July 2002 burned 137,000 acres and destroyed 133 homes and one commercial building (Wilderness Society). The fire resulted from the acts of a Forest Service employee, who was subsequently arrested. Insured losses totaled nearly $80 million, according to the Insurance Services Office (ISO) (Hilbert 2002).

- In northern Arizona, the Rodeo-Chediski fire in June-July 2002, which became Arizona's largest fire ever, burned 463,000 acres, destroyed more than 300 homes, and forced the evacuation of more than 32,000 people. Insurance claims totaled about $120 million, according to the ISO (Hilbert 2002).

The right fuels, the right weather, and a source of ignition can make almost any state the scene of a wildfire.

- Southern California experienced the Old and Grand Prix fires from October 21 to November 4, 2003. By the time these and a dozen other fires were extinguished, the fires had killed 24 people, including one firefighter; injured 246 persons; destroyed 3,631 structures; and burned 739,597 acres in five counties. Damages and response costs exceeded $2 billion, and the effort involved more than 15,000 fire and emergency response personnel (Governor's Blue Ribbon Fire Commission 2004).

A wider survey of the past decade would include other major wildfires in Florida, New York, Alaska, and other states. The right fuels, the right weather, and a source of ignition can make almost any state the scene of a wildfire, even though some regions are clearly more prone to such disasters than others.

WHERE TO BUILD AND HOW

Forest fires have been a part of the natural cycle since long before the dawn of civilization. They are not in and of themselves an environmental problem any more than any other natural phenomenon. As with all natural disasters, the problem lies in the intersection between that phenomenon and the built environment.

The trend toward introducing more of the built environment into fire-prone areas has spawned the modern term "wildland-urban interface" to describe the area where these two forces interact. In order to be useful for scientific and regulatory purposes, such terms need definitions. The official federal definition for wildland-urban interface (WUI) is "the area where structures and other developments meet or intermingle with undeveloped wildland" (USDA and DOI 2001). The *Federal Register* also defines three types of WUI: interface, intermix, and occluded community. The distinctions between these types are discussed below.

James Smalley

Firefighters in Cook City, Wyoming, watch as a wildfire rages in nearby Yellowstone National Park. The 1988 wildfire helped bring the debate over fire suppression policy into public view, with federal officials for the first time publicly questioning the wisdom of the historic policy.

There are few simple answers because the susceptibility of particular areas of WUI to wildfire varies widely both geographically and over time.

The issue that has emerged for planners is how best to manage development in the WUI. There are few simple answers because the susceptibility of particular areas of WUI to wildfire varies widely both geographically and over time. It is important to understand the WUI is a moving target, altered by both natural forces and human intervention.

With that in mind, this PAS Report addresses two issues that may appear to be at cross-purposes:

1. *The wisdom and desirability of permitting development in the forested wildlands where fire is a systemic part of the natural environment.* Some people are now questioning the very idea of building in the WUI because new development exacerbates the problem, often at considerable public expense. Certainly, many more people are questioning unregulated development in such areas. The fires have always been part of the ecosystem, and the need to protect homes compromises those natural cycles, so why build there? Why not establish comprehensive plan policies to direct development to more suitable locations?

2. *How best to design such developments to accomplish a dramatic reduction of the odds of homes being consumed amid wildfires.* This is what happened at the Stevenson Ranch (see sidebar, p. 5). California, hardly the only state experiencing rapid population growth, is adding hundreds of thousands of new residents every year. They must live somewhere. But will finding ways to make their new communities in the wildlands safer serve only to encourage more such development, just as building flood

Table 1-1.
20 Largest California Wildland Fires (By Structures Destroyed)

Fire Name/*Cause*	Date	County	Acres	*Structures*	Deaths
1 Tunnel *(Rekindle)*	October 1991	Alameda	1,600	2,900	25
*2 Cedar *(Human)*	October 2003	San Diego	273,246	2,820	14
*3 Old *(Human)*	October 2003	San Bernardino	91,281	1,003	6
4 Jones *(Undetermined)*	October 1999	Shasta	26,200	954	1
5 Paint *(Arson)*	June 1990	Santa Barbara	4,900	641	1
6 Fountain *(Arson)*	August 1992	Shasta	63,960	636	0
7 City of Berkeley *(Powerlines)*	September 1923	Alameda	130	584	0
8 Bel Air *(Undetermined)*	November 1961	Los Angeles	6,090	484	0
9 Laguna Fire *(Arson)*	October 1993	Orange	14,437	441	0
*10 Paradise *(Human)*	October 2003	San Diego	56,700	415	2
11 Laguna *(Powerlines)*	September 1970	San Diego	175,425	382	5
12 Panorama *(Arson)*	November 1980	San Bernardino	23,600	325	4
13 Topanga *(Arson)*	November 1993	Los Angeles	18,000	323	3
14 49ER *(Burning Debris)*	September 1988	Nevada	33,700	312	0
*15 Simi *(Under Investigation)*	October 2003	Ventura	108,204	300	0
16 Sycamore *(Misc. – Kite)*	July 1977	Santa Barbara	805	234	0
17 Canyon *(Vehicle)*	September 1999	Shasta	2,580	230	0
18 Kannan *(Arson)*	October 1978	Los Angeles	25,385	224	0
19 Kinneloa *(Campfire)*	October 1993	Los Angeles	5,485	196	1
*19 Grand Prix *(Human)*	October 2003	San Bernardino	59,448	196	0
20 Old Gulch *(Equip. Use)*	August 1992	Calaveras	17,386	170	0

Note that this list does not include fire jurisdiction. These are the Top 20 within California, regardless of whether they were state, federal, or local responsibility. Also note that "structures" is meant to include all loss – homes and outbuildings, etc.

(2003 fire statistics to change as final figures are tabulated.)

Source: Ron Montague.

levees sometimes had the effect of encouraging people to build behind them in flood-prone (but seemingly protected) locations? Or is such an analogy even valid in the first place? These questions reprise, in many ways, an ongoing policy discussion in all hazard categories over the comparative degree of emphasis on mitigating hazards in existing development versus avoiding unnecessary levels of risk in new development. Inevitably, it seems, the answer is always we must do as much as possible of both. In addition, planners retain an obligation to protect such natural values as watersheds and wildlife habitat.

This report will not always be able to provide easy answers. The authors describe the best development practices they have identified. In that quest, they are treading a certain line within the ongoing policy debate by discussing *both* comprehensive plan policies and the Firewise design of new subdivisions. No complete discussion of the problem should ignore either side of the equation.

SOUTHERN CALIFORNIA'S SUCCESS STORY

In October 2003, Southern California was once again ablaze. Wildfires swept through nearly 750,000 acres and destroyed more than 3,400 homes (Miller 2003). Before it was over, more than 15,000 firefighters were involved in trying to contain the damage (Governor's Blue Ribbon Fire Commission 2004).

It was hardly the first time, nor would it be the last. The regional ecosystem has evolved with and depends upon a periodic cycle of fire, but since at least the 1950s, Californians have poured into the wooded hills and mountains, and the chaparral landscape of the southern coast in a quest to live closer to nature and its scenic vistas. In regular succession the fires have followed, almost like an annual ritual, right on into the new millennium. Each time, rural subdivisions burned, and homes were lost. It has happened many times, not only in Southern California but in the Bay Area as well. Wildfires have become an integral part of the nation's mental image of California.

Amid the devastation of 2003, however, one development temporarily caught the national news media's attention for a different reason: it failed to burn. Stevenson Ranch was not the only subdivision to survive, and it had some topographical advantages that assisted firefighters. Nonetheless, it seemed good planning had offered the press a positive story, and reporters were eager to know what had gone right.

What the media found in Stevenson Ranch, an unincorporated community of 3,500 homes built since the mid-1990s west of Santa Clarita, were local residents confident of their safety because of measures included under new fire requirements that followed a previous series of wildfires in 1993:
- Windows with double-glazed panes
- Class A assembly roofs
- Moist landscaping[1] and irrigated hillsides cleared of flammable vegetation
- Eaves sealed with stucco to keep sparks out of attics
- Swimming pools equipped with valves to allow use by firefighters
- Oversized address numbers for easy identification

To be sure, local planners will insist these measures improved the odds of survival but do not guarantee it. But that is precisely the point with all natural hazards: mitigation is always a matter of reducing the probabilities of disaster. There are also grounds for questioning whether Stevenson Ranch is the best example or was threatened as seriously as other communities in more vulnerable settings. It also benefited from the intervention of firefighters. Moreover, as the *New York Times* indicated, the development was not without environmental controversy, in large part because it did represent an intrusion of traffic and people into what had been a pristine canyon. There may have been other reasons to debate the desirability of Stevenson Ranch, but the fact remained that not one home was lost. Something had gone right (Murphy 2003).

---

[1] Ron Montague, a technical consultant to the national Firewise program, cautions, however, that while this moist vegetation is effective, "it ignores three important points": 1) Southern California is a desert and imports water, 2) Droughts lead to water restrictions and limited water use, and 3) Irrigated vegetation is more vulnerable when water is limited. In other words, while this solution worked in this case, it may well produce perverse results later, and a better choice might be xeriscaping or the use of less flammable oaks and hardwoods.

Firefighters in a Cook City, Wyoming, diner watch during breakfast as fire rages around Yellowstone National Park in 1988.

James Smalley

WHY PLANNING MATTERS

Wildfire researchers have come to recognize development in the WUI can bring new problems simply by introducing additional people to the interface. Wildfires are more than just a natural hazard and phenomenon. They are also very much a people-triggered hazard, in ways that do not apply to hurricanes, earthquakes, and tornadoes. Humans may not control the weather or geologic processes, but they can and often do control combustion and the flammable materials on which it feeds.

Consider some typical state-level statistics. According to the Washington Department of Natural Resources (WDNR), only a fraction of all wildfires in the state arise from purely natural causes, primarily lightning, which is credited with igniting 13 percent of the fires on WDNR-protected lands. "Protected lands" for which the Washington Department of Natural Resources has responsibility include 12 million acres of both state-owned and privately owned forest lands, as well as 3 million acres of trust lands it manages for the state to provide revenue for construction of schools, other state institutions and prisons, and some county services. Arson accounts for 5.4 percent, recreation for 14 percent, smokers for 5.5 percent, and debris burning for nearly a third (see Figure 1-1). In other words, humans produce most of the sparks that set wildland forests on fire (Washington State Department of Community, Trade and Economic Development 1999). Related statistics from Florida (Figure 1-2) tell much the same story, with 80 percent of fires ignited in some way by humans (Florida DCA and Florida DACS 2004).

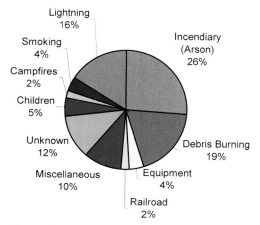

Figure 1-1. Fires on Washington Department of Natural Resources Protected Lands, by Cause

Source: Washington State Department of Community, Trade, and Economic Development 1999.

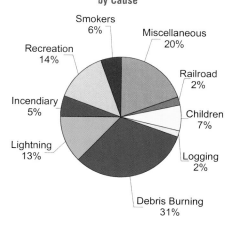

Figure 1-2. Fires in the State of Florida, by Cause

Source: Florida DCA and Florida DACS 2004.

It is essential to understand that a wildfire's origin is irrelevant to its impact. The extent of a wildfire's destruction of life and property will depend far more on the entire series of development decisions, including building design, subdivision design, landscaping and land-use regulations, and management of biological fuel loads. Many of these decisions will have been made years, even decades, before the fire occurred. In fact, the most vital lesson of today's western forest fires is that the historic policy of total suppression of wildfires has led to the buildup of biological fuels that make many current wildfires more severe than would otherwise be the case. Thus, the real point may be that introducing development in some wildland areas complicates the task of mitigating those conditions even as it makes the task more urgent.

The debate over development in fire-prone areas is growing, however, prompted by the intractable realities of building in the WUI, by urgent concerns written into new federal initiatives governing the nation's response to wildfire hazards, and by the steady press of training programs led in large part by Firewise Communities USA. This chapter will discuss all of these issues in turn.

To best understand why planning matters, it is important to review just what the WUI is, how suitable the term is, and where the useful points of strategic planning intervention may lie. The federal government has gone beyond simply establishing the definition ("the area where structures and other developments meet or intermingle with undeveloped wildland") by publishing and updating a comprehensive list of individual communities meeting the definition. The most recent update of this list as of the time of writing this PAS Report was issued in the *Federal Register* in 2001 (Vol. 66:751). It is not necessarily complete, but is the most complete listing the federal government has yet issued, and is a joint product of the U.S. Department of Agriculture's Forest Service and four agencies of the U.S. Department of the Interior (Bureau of Indian Affairs, Bureau of Land Management, Fish and Wildlife Service, and National Park Service).

The two verbs in the federal definition, however, suggest two different possibilities for the interaction between humans and wildland vegetation. It is vital for planners to distinguish between "meet" and "intermingle." The area that meets wildland is "interface," whereas an area where wildland and housing intermingle is "intermix." This may be slightly confusing, given that both types of areas can constitute the WUI, but that is the terminology in use. It is also critical to realize the definition describes not a fixed location but a set of conditions that may exist in a location at one time but not at another. As noted earlier, the WUI is a moving target whose volatility is heavily influenced by fuel types, fuel density and condition, access and egress from developed sites, the choice of building materials, and the density of structures within the area in question.

A 2004 Florida document, *Wildfire Mitigation in Florida*, offers a useful synopsis in this regard. It suggests the so-called "interface" is a more complex mixture of potential situations, depending on topography, forest cover, and other geographical features such as rivers, wetlands, grasslands, and the presence of areas previously cleared for development. As Figure 1-3 shows, only one of three types of interface development truly deserves the designation by actually encompassing development along a border between cleared and forested areas. The area noted as "boundary" in the illustration is equivalent to what the federal definition labels "interface." What the Florida study labels an island is basically an isolated, clearly demarcated sector of wildland fuels, such as a forest preserve within a city. The federal definition refers to this as an "occluded community." Other scattered settlements, often typical of western wildlands development amid hills and mountains, are what Arizona State University professor and fire historian Stephen J. Pyne

The extent of a wildfire's destruction of life and property will depend far more on the entire series of development decisions, including building design, subdivision design, landscaping and land-use regulations, and management of biological fuel loads.

prefers to call "intermix" because there is no clear boundary between homes and forest (Pyne 2004). If anything, the development pattern may more closely resemble a case of chicken pox, with small home-site clearings pockmarking a large forest. Often, these are not even parcels within subdivisions, but simply single homes, frequently perched on hilltops or nestled in private inholdings surrounded by national forest or parkland.

Because the relationship between housing density and forest is an important component of the distinction between types of interface, some researchers have sought to produce an "operational definition" of each type of WUI that can be used as a practical method of classifying communities. Susan Stewart (2004), a research physical scientist with the United States Department of Agriculture (USDA) Forest Service's Northeast Research Station in Evanston, Illinois, reports "intermix and interface are concepts that work well when using subunits of communities; one can refer to a census block or neighborhood as being intermix/interface type WUI. An occluded community does not translate well to the fine scale of our data . . . so we dropped it." What Stewart and her colleagues have been trying to achieve is an "operational" definition of WUI types to classify actual communities or community areas. "We feel that this resolution is a useful and important feature of the data, which has utility for planners," she adds.

In their operational definition, interface areas contain more than one house per 16 hectares (roughly 6.5 acres), less than 50 percent vegetation, located within 1.5 miles of an area over 500 hectares (a little more than 200 acres) that is more than 75 percent vegetated. Stewart explains that this distance "has a bit more empirical basis, in that the California Fire Authority uses 1.5 miles as its estimate of the distance a firebrand can carry on the wind," a means of determining where houses may be in danger. Intermix areas have more than one house per 16 hectares but more than 50 percent vegetation. Higher-density housing is more characteristic of the interface than of the intermix, but the latter is more extensive, comprising 82 percent of WUI land area in the United States (Stewart, Radeloff, and Hammer 2003).

Figure 1-3. Categories of Wildland-Urban Interface

There are three major categories of wildland-urban interface. Depending on the set of conditions present, any of these areas may be at risk from wildfire. A wildfire risk assessment can determine the level of risk.

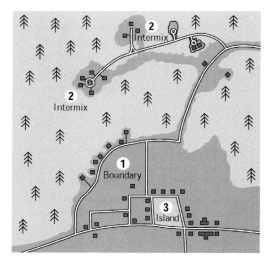

1. **"Boundary" wildland-urban interface** is characterized by areas of development where homes, especially new subdivisions, press against public and private wildlands, such as private or commercial forest land or public forests and parks. This is the classic type of wildland-urban interface, with a clearly defined boundary between the suburban fringe and the rural countryside.

2. **"Intermix" wildland-urban interface** areas are places where improved property and/or structures are scattered and interspersed in wildland areas. These may be isolated rural homes or an area that is just beginning to go through the transition from rural to urban land uses.

3. **"Island" wildland-urban interface,** also called "occluded" interface, are areas of wildland within predominantly urban or suburban areas. As cities or subdivisions grow, islands of undeveloped land may remain, creating remnant forests. Sometimes these remnants exist as parks, or as land that cannot be developed due to site limitations, such as wetlands.

Source: Florida DCA and Florida DACS 2004.

In addition to delineating three types of WUI, the Florida study offers three intellectual perspectives: sociopolitical, biophysical, and fire management. The first sees the interface as a battleground between opposing views concerning the value of open space and the development potential of such lands. The second views the interface as an area undergoing changes in forest ecosystems as a result of the encroachment of urban development, including such ecological shifts as changes in stormwater runoff and soil erosion, habitat fragmentation, and the arrival of invasive species. Finally, fire management considers the area in terms of the intermingling of structures with vegetative fuels, the potential for the structures themselves to become fuels that heighten the fire risk, and issues involving emergency response, such as access and weather conditions (Florida DCA and Florida DACS 2004).

The danger is that the experts, local officials, and citizens who consider the problem from these varying perspectives may amount to so many blind men feeling the elephant unless they are brought together in an effort to develop a larger, more comprehensive picture of the problem. The issue of development in the WUI is not just any one of these issues; it is all of them in dynamic and evolving combination. Decisions made about permitting development affect the viability of firefighting and emergency response. Decisions made with firefighting in mind affect the capital budget of the jurisdiction that must invest in the necessary infrastructure and capacity to handle the job. All of these decisions affect the quantity and quality of stormwater runoff, particularly in areas with steep topography, and all may affect wildland habitats of native species.

Planners have a major role to play in all these decisions, but they cannot enter the arena uneducated. They must learn the different perspectives about the interface as well as the basic science and terminology. Toward that end, Chapters 2 and 3 present, respectively, the history of the U.S. experience with wildfires and the known science of their behavior. Once planners have mastered the essentials, they are in an excellent position to help lead the participants in this debate to understand this complex web. They can facilitate compromises in some instances, stand their ground on some issues, and help reach conclusions about what works and when, where, and how the community will allow specific kinds of development. Many of the issues are similar to those planners have confronted in other contexts: the extension of infrastructure, managing growth, stormwater management, open space preservation, and subdivision design, among others. It is a matter not of reinventing the wheel, but of adapting it. Chapter 4 will digest and evaluate local wildfire plans and regulations. Chapter 5 concludes with a discussion of the big issues in wildfire planning, and the stakes they entail.

Planners have a major role to play in all these decisions, but they cannot enter the arena uneducated.

TRENDS IN WUI DEVELOPMENT

Some states face serious problems with the proliferation of development in wildfire-prone areas at least in part because of population growth. Others confront the problem largely as a matter of choices made by homeowners and builders. In addition, historic settlement patterns, especially those in the Rocky Mountain states, often complicate land-use planning to mitigate wildfire hazards. Most notable among these are homesteading claims, old mining claims, and the checkerboard pattern of inholdings, which are individual parcels scattered within national forest lands, national parklands, and Native American tribal reservations. The tribal checkerboard patterns often resulted from attempts in the late nineteenth century to place white farmers within tribal lands in a frequently misguided effort to transfer their agricultural skills and work ethic to their neighbors (Kickingbird and Ducheneaux 1973). These pre-existing development rights heighten the challenge for rural and county planners seeking to reduce the community's exposure to wildfire hazards.

California and Florida are clearly the best-known examples of states with significant wildfire hazards experiencing population pressures, although they are not alone. In percentage terms, the five fastest-growing states between 1990 and 2000 were Nevada (66.3 percent), Arizona (40 percent), Colorado (30.6 percent), Utah (29.6 percent), and Idaho (28.5 percent). All are states with demonstrable wildfire hazards. In sheer numbers, however, California (which grew 13.8 percent) is adding the equivalent of a city the size of Fresno every year. Florida grew by more than 3 million people (23.5 percent) between 1990 and 2000, to nearly 16 million residents, challenging New York for its third-place status (U.S. Census Bureau 2001). Historically, most of Florida's population has always lived near the coast, an area with its own significant hazard considerations due to coastal storms. The added population is now engendering growth toward the interior, overtaking heavily forested areas with a natural history of adaptation to wildfire. In addition, notes Jeffrey Bielling, principal planner with the Florida Department of Community Affairs, much of the forested land in the state's interior belongs to timber companies that are now becoming developers, subdividing and reselling the land (Bielling 2004).

Moreover, the new residents often have short histories in the Sunshine State and understand little of its ecology (Florida DCA and Florida DACS 2004). The result is a serious lack of fit between their imported behavioral patterns and the fire-adapted landscape of Florida's interior. Without massive and ongoing education, a daunting task being undertaken by Florida's local and state development agencies and fire officials, the combination of these forces is, and sometimes in recent years has been, a recipe for disaster. The massive wildfires of 1998 that seized the attention of the national news media are merely a harbinger of things to come.

The United States is a diverse country, however. The western states and Florida represent one extreme end of a spectrum of population and development pressures that affect trends with respect to the WUI. To one extent or another, some type of WUI development exists in every state. Stewart, Radeloff, and Hammer (2003) have attempted to map this distribution; Table 1-2 is their documentation of the extent of WUI development across the U.S. Table 1-3 lists in order the five leading states in terms of four categories—total area, percentage of overall state area, number of homes, and percentage of homes—within the interface, intermix, and total WUI respectively. In other words, North Carolina has the largest acreage of both intermix and total WUI, but not of interface, while California has the largest number of homes both in the WUI as a whole and within both types of WUI specifically. It is important to know that the data in these two tables represent an adaptation of the criteria outlined in the *Federal Register* by the five agencies responsible for managing wildland fire problems, based on the authors' development of the operational definitions of types of WUI described above.

It is important to differentiate the significance of these rankings as they relate to wildfire hazards. For instance, the high ranking of the District of Columbia, at 19 percent, in area of interface, or even of Rhode Island in area of intermix at 61 percent, does not at all indicate a problem of the same magnitude as one might find in California or even Pennsylvania. The D.C. numbers simply reflect the presence of a healthy urban forest and park system, but one whose wildfire threat is surely manageable by the local fire department. In many rural areas of the nation, however, local fire departments, often volunteer in nature, are easily overwhelmed

California and Florida are clearly the best-known examples of states with significant wildfire hazards experiencing population pressures, although they are not alone.

Table 1-2.
Land Area and Houses in Interface and Intermix, Conterminous United States

| | Land Area | | | Percent of all |
	(hectares)	(percent)	Houses	U.S. Houses
Interface				
High density	760,243	5.9%	10,665,201	9.3%
Medium density	4,031,381	31.4%	9,636,597	8.4%
Low density	8,046,870	62.7%	1,339,869	1.2%
Total interface	12,838,493	100%	21,641,666	18.8%
Percent of WUI	18.1%			
Intermix				
High density	186,030	0.3%	2,552,907	2.2%
Medium density	7,680,518	13.2%	10,379,554	9.0%
Low density	50,165,498	86.4%	7,723,636	6.7%
Total Intermix	58,032,047	100%	20,656,097	17.9%
Percent of WUI	81.9%			
Total WUI	70,870,539	9.3%	42,297,763	36.7%
All U.S.	765,647,714	100%	115,183,121	100%

High density housing: >7.5 Housing Units/ha; medium: >1 HU/2ha to 7.5 HU/ha; low: >1 HU/16 ha to 1 HU/2 ha.

Source: Stewart, Radeloff, and Hammer 2003.

Table 1-3.
State Rank by Area and Homes in Interface, Intermix and Total WUI

	Rank	Interface		Intermix		WUI	
Area (ha)							
	1	PA	1,047,996	NC	4,784,799	NC	5,168,959
	2	CA	746,037	GA	3,328,643	PA	4,338,163
	3	NY	707,520	PA	3,290,167	GA	3,647,157
	4	TN	594,908	VA	2,911,322	NY	3,573,620
	5	VA	592,546	NY	2,866,100	VA	3,503,868
Area (percent)							
	1	DC	19%	RI	61%	CT	72%
	2	NJ	15%	CT	60%	RI	69%
	3	CT	12%	MA	53%	MA	65%
	4	MA	12%	NH	38%	NJ	46%
	5	PA	9%	NC	38%	NH	41%
Homes (number)							
	1	CA	3,480,285	CA	1,607,624	CA	5,087,909
	2	PA	1,394,977	GA	1,479,368	PA	2,541,343
	3	FL	1,169,090	NC	1,451,811	TX	2,310,811
	4	NY	996,583	PA	1,146,366	FL	1,947,409
	5	MA	982,921	TX	1,141,721	NC	1,776,212
Homes (percent)							
	1	WY	62%	ME	50%	NH	82%
	2	NM	41%	NH	47%	WV	80%
	3	MT	40%	GA	45%	WY	80%
	4	UT	40%	WV	42%	ME	79%
	5	WV	38%	NC	41%	NM	79%

Source: Stewart, Radeloff, and Hammer 2003.

by major forest fires. Federal and state resources are almost inevitably summoned in such disasters.

While the problem of wildfires is national in scope, the nature of the hazard is not identical from one region to another. In the Southeast, particularly in semitropical Florida, frequent rains more often than not serve as a deterrent to serious wildfires, but the sheer quantity of vegetation the climate produces can be a prescription for catastrophe when the rare drought occurs, as it did in 1998. That makes managing the fuel load in the interface an absolutely essential component of mitigation. On the other hand, Florida faces none of the issues of access through steep slopes and mountains that bedevil fire management in the Rocky Mountains or California, and the density of development in most cases augurs well for an abundance of firefighting resources, while the absence of such in more rural states often forces reliance on outside aid. Forest health can also vary widely, with some states like Arizona coping with dangerous quantities of dead and dying vegetation as a result of such threats as infestations of bark beetles. Moreover, western states, unlike the East, have land-ownership patterns dominated by large federal holdings and tribal reservations within which growth management may be complicated by old patterns of inholdings, as noted above. In short, strategies for mitigation, including land-use controls, must respond to the specific circumstances of the community, state, and region. No one solution fits all.

Historically, in fact, the largest wildfires in U.S. history occurred in the upper Midwest, in states with large logging operations like Michigan, Wisconsin, and Minnesota. As Chapter 2 will show, those days are largely over, but the potential for serious fires in a period of prolonged drought remains. The Midwest, however, is blessed with a much less arid climate, so prolonged droughts are relatively rare. On the other hand, in a climate fostering vegetative growth at far greater densities than is common in most of the West, the potential for catastrophe should meteorological patterns change is something that planners, firefighters, and foresters must all regard with caution. Florida, precisely because of its humid, in part semitropical, climate, fosters rampant vegetative growth, much of it containing species that burn easily and rapidly, such as palmetto. When a prolonged drought amid hot weather occurs, as happened in 1998, the sheer volume of dead and dying vegetation creates a tinderbox unlike any that can possibly accumulate in the Rocky Mountains. The only roughly comparable settings for wildfires occur in the Pacific Northwest, where a lush temperate rainforest extends along the coast from Northern California into British Columbia and the Alaskan panhandle.

As intriguing as the data may be, they have some distinct limitations. The definition that enables the mapping behind these statistics is only a few years old; hence, no comparable statistics were developed in prior years to show a progression over time in the development of the interface or the precise extent of its growth. Data collection is still somewhat fragmented. There remains a great deal of work to do in defining who already lives in, and who is moving to, the interface, and why. Most importantly, the nature of the WUI and the challenges it poses vary significantly from one region to another and sometimes even within the same state. As a result, defining the severity of the problem in a specific area and deciding what measures will be most effective in mitigating the hazard remain very local and regional functions. The ideal measures will be different even between Colorado and Arizona, let alone between Florida and Oregon. There is much work for planners and others to do, and much of it will necessarily take place in individual communities and counties across the nation.

While the problem of wildfires is national in scope, the nature of the hazard is not identical from one region to another.

WHY PEOPLE BUILD AND LIVE IN THE WUI

Living in the WUI clearly can be risky business. Fortunately, there is a growing body of sociological and demographic literature exploring the question of how people make the tradeoffs, consciously or otherwise, that lead to their decision to live in locations that entail wildfire hazards.

There is not a direct correlation between locating in the WUI and facing a wildfire hazard. Much of what is defined as the WUI does not face significant wildfire risks. The risks vary by region; some areas experience much more frequent problems than others. Although any wooded area is potentially the site of a wildfire, there are areas where the threat is sufficiently minimal and infrequent to justify landowners' expectations that they can enjoy the natural amenity without undue concern. In other locations, the certainty of periodic—and severe—wildfire hazards is so great as to raise serious questions about the wisdom of permitting development there. Also, wildfire dangers are not limited to the woods, but can include grasslands and shrub, such as California's notoriously combustible chaparral.

Although specific attractions are more numerous, social scientists exploring the demographics of the WUI have tended to identify what might be called the "big three" reasons for homeowners' attraction to the forest: (1) nature, (2) wildlife, and (3) privacy (Nelson et al. 2002). Nan Johnson (2004), a planner with the Colorado State Forest Service, suggests a fourth consideration: the call of the rugged, nonurban lifestyle. These attractions are among the primary magnets in a broader phenomenon that sociologists call "amenity migration," the tendency to relocate to an area because of its environmental or cultural features rather than for economic reasons (Johnson and Beale 2002; Vasievich 1999).

Nature

The desire to be "close to nature," however, begs the question of what constitutes any individual's perceptions of nature. Clearly, for most, it involves some degree of removal from the built environment, except to the extent that they bring a small part of it with them by building a home in the woods, and a closer proximity to flora, fauna, and perhaps landscape features such as creeks, waterfalls, or mountains. The individual mixture of ingredients, however, is highly subjective, as is the word "nature" itself. For some, the attachment to nature forbids any consideration of human intervention to reduce wildfire hazards through mitigation efforts, such as prescribed burns, forest thinning, or other types of vegetation management. For others, all of these measures may be acceptable as long as the surrounding landscape remains fundamentally undeveloped. These perceptions often have little historical foundation with respect to the prior treatment of the landscape involved. In Florida, for example, many developments in the inland woods arise on lands formerly owned by timber companies as plantations. Many other areas in the Northeast and Midwest now have second- or third-growth forest after decades of logging activity. Residents may be unaware these landscapes have undergone such significant transformations under prior human influence.

Wildlife

The desire to witness wildlife in one's backyard and beyond may be somewhat less problematic. Wildlife comes in many forms, some of which adapt extremely well to the human presence, others of which thrive better at a distance. The former include some animals that thrive almost too well in combination with encroaching development—raccoons and squirrels, for example. Wildlife lovers often have educated themselves on means of manipulating the attractions for various species, especially birds, to

Social scientists exploring the demographics of the WUI have tended to identify what might be called the "big three" reasons for homeowners' attraction to the forest: (1) nature, (2) wildlife, and (3) privacy.

enhance the experiences of those who love to observe them. Bird feeders are an obvious example.

Development in the interface, however, also affects the presence and quality of wildlife in many subtle ways less readily recognized by those who live there. Buildings and subdivisions can fragment habitat, relocating the wildland edge and the species that thrive there (such as deer), and perhaps favoring other species that prefer open ground (such as quail). These factors may not mar the quality of the experience for wildlife lovers, but the changes in the landscape will most certainly affect the composition of the wildlife they observe. The precise nature of the impact depends a great deal on the local ecosystem.

Privacy

Privacy may or may not work in combination with the two environmental values. It is rooted in a desire to withdraw, either from civilization generally or at least to some degree from the prying eyes of neighbors, and may work against any efforts to encourage defensible space around a home. People seeking a great deal of privacy in the WUI may view large trees and extensive vegetation as a means of obscuring their presence and making activities less visible or audible.

Rugged Lifestyle

The lure of a challenging, rugged lifestyle has been a part of the American culture and legacy at least as far back as Daniel Boone. It would seem a logical assumption that it is more closely related to the locational choices of people who choose remote individual homesites than to the decisions of middle-class or affluent families to move into well-cultivated new subdivisions in the WUI full of modern amenities. This lifestyle choice, however, is a real phenomenon in many rural areas, particularly those with mountainous terrain, such as Appalachia or the Rocky Mountains.

Attractions aside, however, people have more often chosen locations for economic reasons than for sentimental ones. People traditionally have needed to be close to jobs. In rural settings, employment most often involved either agriculture or extractive industries like mining and logging. The big shift of recent decades, in which formerly depopulating rural areas have attracted newcomers, has resulted from changes in technology that have allowed people to live and work at home, away from cities, through telecommunications and computers (Johnson and Beale 1998). The ability to live where one wishes rather than where one must, combined with growing numbers of retirees who are no longer economically tethered to urban areas, will almost surely reshape development pressures for decades to come and compound the challenge of regulating development in hazard-prone areas.

FEDERAL INITIATIVES

As wildfires have continued to seize national attention, federal initiatives have moved beyond training and education to statutory mandates and greater programmatic efforts. Unlike those connected with many other hazards, however, the efforts connected to wildfires have largely evolved outside the regulatory framework controlled by the Federal Emergency Management Agency (FEMA). Although FEMA does contain the U.S. Fire Administration, that agency has historically focused on urban rather than wildland fire. Instead, with the U.S. Forest Service in the lead, wildfire programs have largely been the domain of a consortium of federal agencies involved in the management of federal lands, including the Bureau of Land Management (BLM), the Bureau of Indian Affairs, the National Park

As wildfires have continued to seize national attention, federal initiatives have moved beyond training and education to statutory mandates and greater programmatic efforts.

Service, and the Fish and Wildlife Service. As might be expected, their relationship with the communities most affected by their approach to the problem is most often that of a big neighbor whose every decision affects the welfare of adjoining local jurisdictions. Under those circumstances, it is vital for all parties—federal, state, and local—to learn the tools and lessons of building effective partnerships to address the wildland fire problem.

The 2000 wildfire season, which included the Cerro Grande fire that destroyed 235 homes in Los Alamos, New Mexico, ended with an urgent report by the Council of Western State Foresters recommending greater federal attention to problems created by development in wildlands. Prodded by these recommendations, Congress in 2001 asked the Forest Service and the Department of the Interior to underwrite what became a series of studies by the National Academy of Public Administration exploring ways of restraining federal expenditures for suppressing wildfires. The initial reports dealt with the management of wildfire suppression operations, but by 2003 the Academy undertook an examination of the ways in which wildfire mitigation could assist in cost containment. In a noteworthy effort to condense the message, the final report included a graphic (Figure 1-4) summarizing the "hand" with which local officials and WUI residents could play, depending on the wildfire mitigation efforts they had undertaken (NAPA 2004). Slowly but inexorably, in recent years, largely driven by budgetary concerns, the emphasis at the federal level is shifting from responding to disasters to mitigating their impact beforehand. That shift is, in turn, altering the relationship of the relevant federal agencies with local and state governments. In time, it is inevitable that this new relationship will also result in greater accountability on the part of local governments for the consequences of the patterns of development they permit.

Figure 1-4. Wildfire Hazard Mitigation is Essential

- When fire breaks out, you play the hand you've been dealt

- Which hand would you prefer?

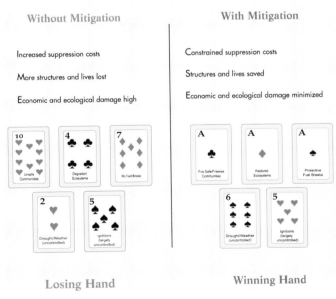

Source: National Academy of Public Administration 2004.

In the wake of this emphasis in federal activity, President Bush in December 2003 signed into law the Healthy Forests Restoration Act (P.L. 108-148). Many environmentalists fear a bonanza for timber companies because the law opens up non-WUI forestlands for thinning in order to reduce forest fire dangers, but it also contains one major provision driving multiagency planning, particularly in cooperation with communities neighboring BLM and Forest Service lands, to enhance wildfire mitigation. The new law steps up federal support for fuel reduction efforts to $760 million, not just on federal lands but also on state, private, and tribal lands.

One important feature of the law is the priority consideration it affords to fuel reduction on nonfederal lands if they are identified in collaboratively developed Community Wildfire Protection Plans (CWPP). These plans are helping forge the partnership envisioned between the Forest Service and local governments. This mechanism provides a significant opportunity for productive partnership in managing the problem, one that some states have seized. The Colorado State Forest Service, for example, is investing considerable effort in helping communities to develop such plans (Johnson 2004). It may help that the state agency already had a statutory designation in state enabling legislation to provide technical assistance to local government in the preparation of comprehensive plan elements addressing wildfire hazards (Schwab 2002).

The first wave of community wildfire protection plans began to emerge in late 2004. In October 2004, the Greater Flagstaff Forests Partnership (GFFP) with the Ponderosa Fire Advisory Council in Arizona released its final draft plan (see GFFP and PFAC 2004). GFFP is an alliance of 26 environmental and governmental organizations, including the Forest Service, "dedicated to researching and demonstrating approaches to forest ecosystem restoration in the ponderosa pine forests surrounding Flagstaff" (www.gffp.org).

The first wave of community wildfire protection plans began to emerge in late 2004.

Another model exists in Oregon, where Andre LeDuc, professor of urban planning at the University of Oregon, has been heading a unique statewide outreach and education partnership at the Community Service Center's Oregon Natural Hazards Workgroup. The program seeks to move beyond regulations alone to assisting with the creation of a wider palette of local and homeowner options for addressing wildfire hazards (LeDuc 2004).

What matters is that the CWPPs have become a means for engaging citizens and local officials in confronting the problem. It is all part of a far broader trend with regard to planning and federal involvement in hazard mitigation. In combination with the new local mitigation strategies required for eligibility for mitigation grants under the Disaster Mitigation Act of 2000 (P.L. 106-390), as well as hazard-related elements required or recommended in local comprehensive plans under some state growth management regimes, the CWPPs are part of a widening effort to move beyond the cycle of build-disaster-rebuild with all types of natural hazards at all levels of government. In that effort, challenges lay ahead, including that of integrating the FEMA grants, programs, and requirements with those emanating from other federal agencies (NAPA 2004). Nonetheless, wildfires are rapidly assuming their own major place in the pantheon of hazard-related local planning concerns.

THE IMPACT OF FIREWISE

The nation's primary outreach program for training communities to deal comprehensively with wildfires grew out of a bad fire season in Florida in 1985 that wiped out 600 homes (Florida DCA and Florida DACS 2004). Firewise, managed by the National Fire Protection Association (NFPA),

PARTNERSHIPS FOR HEALTHY FORESTS

A central idea behind the Community Wildfire Protection Plan envisioned in the Healthy Forests Protection Act is the development of partnerships that involve a wide range of stakeholders. The Flagstaff plan exhibits a model of such involvement with widespread stakeholder participation. As of September 2004, the two coordinating entities for the plan listed the following advisory board members:

Greater Flagstaff Forests Partnership
Arizona Game & Fish
Arizona Public Service
Arizona State Land Department—Fire
Management Division
City of Flagstaff—Fire Department
Coconino County—Community
Development Department
Coconino County Farm Bureau/Cattle
Growers Association
Coconino Natural Resource
Conservation District
Coconino Rural Environment Corps
Cocopai Resource Conservation &
Development District
Ecological Restoration Institute at
Northern Arizona University
Flagstaff Chamber of Commerce
Flagstaff Native Plant & Seed
Grand Canyon Trust
Greater Flagstaff Economic Council
H & K Consulting
Highlands Fire District (Communities
of Kachina Village, Forest Highlands
and Mountainaire)
Indigenous Community Enterprises
Northern Arizona University—College
of Engineering
Northern Arizona University—School
of Forestry
Perkins Timber Harveesting
Ponderosa Fire Advisory Council

Practical Mycology
Southwest Environmental Consultants
Society of American Foresters—
Northern Arizona Chapter
The Arboretum at Flagstaff
The Nature Conservancy
U.S. Fish and Wildlife Service

Cooperators
USDA Coconino National Forest
USDA Rocky Mountain, Pacific NW
and Southern Research Stations
USDA Forest Products Lab

Ponderosa Fire Advisory Council
Arizona State Land Department
Camp Navajo Fire Department
Coconino County Emergency Services
Coconino National Forest
Coconino Sheriff Department
Flagstaff Fire Department
Flagstaff Police Department
Flagstaff Ranch Fire Department
Highlands Fire Department
Kaibab National Forest
Mormon Lake Fire Department
Parks/Bellemont Fire Department
Pinewood Fire Department
Sedona Fire Department
Summit Fire Department
Walnut Canyon-Wapatki-Sunset Crater
National Monuments

evolved as a cooperative effort supported by several federal agencies, including the USDA Forest Service, the U.S. Department of the Interior, and the National Association of State Foresters. It eventually spawned Firewise Communities, a nationwide series of three-day workshops, the first of which was held in Deerfield Beach, Florida, in October 1999. That program, in turn, gave birth to Firewise Communities/USA, which certifies communities that meet its standards for mitigating local wildfire hazards (see sidebar).

Florida Division of Forestry

The 1998 wildfire season spurred the state of Florida to become an early participant in the national Firewise Communities training workshops.

FIREWISE COMMUNITIES/USA CERTIFICATION IN FIVE STEPS

The Firewise Web site lists five steps for communities to achieve certification as a Firewise Community/USA:

- Enlist a WUI specialist to complete a community assessment and create a plan that identifies agreed-upon achievable solutions to be implemented by the community.
- Sponsor a local Firewise Task Force Committee, Commission, or Department that maintains the Firewise Community/USA program and tracks its progress or status.
- Observe a Firewise Communities/USA Day each spring dedicated to a local Firewise project.
- Invest a minimum of $2.00 per capita annually in local Firewise projects. (Work by municipal employees or volunteers using municipal and other equipment can be included, as can state/federal grants dedicated to that purpose.)
- Submit an annual report to Firewise Communities/USA documenting continuing compliance with the program.

Firewise Communities/USA is a project of the National Wildfire Coordinating Group's Wildland/Urban Interface Working Team and is the newest element of the Firewise program. For further program information, check the Firewise Communities/USA Web site at www.firewise.org/usa/.

By the summer of 2003, Firewise Communities had conducted 25 workshops across the nation, training more than 1,200 participants from 47 states. The mixture of participants varied from one location to another but included an interdisciplinary assortment of foresters, firefighters, urban planners, elected officials, architects, homeowners association representatives, and others. The diversity of the audience reflects the comprehensiveness of the discussion needed in most communities affected by wildfire hazards. After three years of workshops, Firewise contracted with APA to conduct an assessment of the impact this training had produced in the communities from which the participants came (Schwab, Ross, and Walther 2003). A key purpose of the training was to expand the public awareness of wildfire mitigation to include issues of better land-use planning and greater responsibility by WUI homeowners for minimizing their own risks.

Five years after its inception, the Firewise training program can justly take a major share of the credit for fostering a sense that homeowners, instead of being victims saved by firefighters, needed to become partners by taking a variety of steps not only to reduce the flammability of their own structures but also increasing the ability of firefighters to defend those structures. Those measures included changes in building materials and clearing of fire-prone brush. Firewise also built into its training GIS-based interactive workshops in which participants learned to analyze, from a planning perspective, the strengths and weaknesses of a proposed subdivision in a fire-prone landscape. This hands-on exercise later formed the basis of one of three hazard scenarios built into a one-day hazard mitigation planning course, "Planning for a Disaster-Resistant Community," developed by APA for FEMA. The course remains available to any entity willing to host it. Firewise staff assisted in that process. In addition, Firewise spawned a series of state-level imitators, often managed by state forestry departments and lasting one day rather than three. These had the advantage of significantly extending the outreach of the original program to local communities and regional planning councils.

One of the most ambitious state efforts materialized early on in Florida, managed by the Florida Division of Forestry. Between August 2000 and the publication of this PAS Report, Florida had conducted 25 workshops of its own. It trained 1,073 participants, an estimated 10 percent of them planners or appointed planning officials, the others including foresters, firefighters, and elected or appointed officials (Harrell 2004). Several large jurisdictions have adopted wildfire mitigation plans, including Indian River and Okechobee counties. Florida was far from alone. Since the national Firewise workshop series was phased out in December 2003, a growing number of other states, such as Colorado, New Mexico, and Arizona, have been producing their own versions.

CHAPTER 2

Historical Overview of Wildfires in the U.S.

nowing how we created our situation requires some knowledge of where we have been. An excellent and growing body of literature on the history of wildfires and forests in both North America and the world allows a greater understanding of the relationship between human use of the land and the way in which nature responds. This chapter reviews that history to create a framework for reshaping the directions in which American development of the wildland-urban interface (WUI) is now headed.

What may emerge for readers from a familiarity with this history is some sense of "been there, done that," but also an awareness that, while we have learned a great deal about coping with wildfire challenges in our nation's wildlands, we are still deeply engaged in a learning curve with a very wide arc. Hard-learned lessons of the past are prelude to new lessons being learned in the present and still awaiting us in the future. The one inescapable conclusion of the history of North American wildfires is that our collective behavior in managing our forests and other wildlands directly affects our potential for experiencing disasters in the WUI.

EARLY HISTORY OF THE FRONTIER

People and fire have been inseparable elements of the world's natural landscape for millennia. Without the human presence, wildfires are largely a phenomenon generated by lightning, which has its own natural cycle. Nature reduces the forest fuel load at its own pace, fostering the germination and growth of certain fire-dependent species at the expense of others in a bewildering variety of local ecosystems.

While we have learned a great deal about coping with wildfire challenges in our nation's wildlands, we are still deeply engaged in a learning curve with a very wide arc.

Since prehistoric times, humans have established their own role in the natural system. They have found a number of ways to reshape the environment to their own benefit. They have used fire to hold the forest at bay, to carve out pastureland for domesticated livestock, and to foster the growth of prairie grasslands and well-cleared forests to facilitate hunting and to espy the approach of enemies from a distance (Pyne 2001). It is now well established that almost all Native American societies in North America used fire for one or more of these purposes. Far from being untouched by human hands, the environment that Europeans discovered as they moved across the continent was in fact profoundly influenced by the use of fire by indigenous peoples. In contrast to the American mythology of settlers carving farms out of the forested wilderness, those in the Midwest, in particular, often saw the forest encroach on the grasslands they had divided up and converted to farms. Having erected wooden fences, barns, and homes, they resisted the Native American use of fire, which had burned back the saplings, and the new growth sprung up before them. Farming and wildfires made poor companions (Cronon 1992).

What is important about this initial sequence—although greatly oversimplified here—is that both Native Americans and European settlers made distinct impacts on the North American landscape, each in their own way. That is not to say that the impacts were equivalent, but both were substantial. Native Americans for the most part treated fire as a tool, one often reserved to specific members of the tribe who had learned how to use it wisely (FEMA 2004). Europeans, on the other hand, saw the forest largely as a resource to be exploited. As the American nation expanded westward, building homes and cities along the way, the need for lumber spawned large timbering operations in those areas where the woods were abundant, while farms carved up those portions of the land that were amenable to agriculture. Cities grew, logically enough, in those locations that had access to waterways, even after the advent of the railroad. Vast quantities of timber moved across the Great Lakes and down the Mississippi River and its tributaries.

THE "GREAT BARBECUE"

Initially, Americans brought little experience to the task of managing the environment of the vast forests they sought to log. At the same time, they were not particularly receptive to Native American wisdom, which was largely regarded as primitive. In the upper Midwest, especially, but elsewhere as well, the stage was set for a repetitive national disaster that fire historian Stephen J. Pyne calls "the Great Barbecue," a phrase he attributes to historian V.L. Parrington (Pyne 1982). Lumbering operations left significant quantities of kindling in their wake despite what we might now regard as obvious dangers. Railroads, rapidly expanding into the nation's interior, often to provide transportation for the raw product the sawmills provided, provided sparks that, in hot, dry weather, sometimes started conflagrations that quickly spun out of control. It happened over and over, with devastation on a scale difficult to imagine today.

Nature's first warning shot was a loud one. While most Americans are aware of the Great Chicago Fire in 1871, few are aware it was anything but an isolated disaster. Mythology about Mrs. O'Leary's cow notwithstanding, the fire broke out on exactly the same day, October 8, that wildfires occurred elsewhere throughout the Midwest, stemming from prolonged hot, dry summer throughout the region. The drought had converted a surplus of sawdust, slash, forest debris, and the lumber itself into a powder keg of fuel lying in wait for some sparks. Chicago, using the railroads to build its economy as the lumberyard to the Midwest and the East, gained more attention merely because it was a growing urban center with easy access to the nation's news media. Reports of its catastrophe spread more quickly to the outside world.

At the same time, however, one of the worst wildfires in U.S. history was burning through northeastern Wisconsin near the logging community of Peshtigo, north of Green Bay. Killing at least 1,500 people, a wall of flames five miles wide scorched a landscape exceeding 2,400 square miles. So intense were the flames that they spawned their own tornado-like winds in their wake, giving the English language a new word, "firestorm," as survivors struggled to describe the holocaust they had experienced. Many of them, immigrants who had followed the railroads west in search of jobs in the logging camps, would never overcome their horror at what they had seen. It was the nation's sobering introduction to the unanticipated consequences of its breakneck expansion into the woods. Other fires had spread across parts of Minnesota during the same week. North Dakota saw some small towns wiped off the map.

Even then, a few visionary scientists knew that the disasters were clearly related. The disaster made the case for Increase Lapham, who pioneered the science of connecting the impacts of severe meteorological patterns and the misuse of the land. In 1867, he had published a prescient work, *Report on the Disastrous Effects of the Destruction of Forest Trees Now Going on in the State of Wisconsin*. His work became integral to the creation of the nation's first weather agency under the Department of War in 1870, providing the first means to telegraph storm warnings based on systematic observations (Gess and Lutz 2002).

The inferno in Peshtigo was merely the first in a series of such calamities spread over the next half century. Hampered by a dearth of science on the subject and the lack of modern firefighting equipment, detached from indigenous forest fire wisdom by an antipathy toward Native American culture, America lurched forward into one wildfire after another, typically in the upper Midwest where extractive industries had created the conditions in which fire could thrive. The actual causes were multiple, and the precise source of ignition was in retrospect probably a secondary consideration: sparks from passing trains, land-clearing fires begun by farmers carving out a homestead in the wake of the loggers, a campfire here and there. The modern forensics for determining such things were lacking in any case.

And so the wildfires came. Major fires occurred in Michigan in 1881. Minnesota, Wisconsin, and Michigan hosted fires in 1894, and again in 1908. Again, in 1911, Michigan had the Ausable wildfires. And yet again, in 1918, Michigan and Minnesota suffered (Pyne 1982). This last episode, centered

While most Americans are aware of the Great Chicago Fire in 1871, few are aware it was anything but an isolated disaster.

in the northern sawmill town of Cloquet, Minnesota, took 450 lives and burned 250,000 acres. It may not have been on the same scale as Peshtigo, but it provided a ghoulish bookend to an era that had lasted long enough.

When one examines the National Interagency Fire Center's inventory of historically significant fires of the latter half of the twentieth century (Table 2-1), there is a notable change following the "Great Barbecue" to an era in which the geographic location, the loss of life, and the sheer size of wildfires all shift. Fires became less lethal and, with some exceptions, less vast. More significantly, the heavy logging era of the upper Midwest came to a close, and the fire problem moved west at the very time when the conservation movement took hold politically and began to reshape the nation's concept of forestry from one of exploitation to that of responsible stewardship.

Nonetheless, many mining towns in the West experienced repetitive burning and rebuilding, taking obvious risks in stride and laying the foundations of many rural communities that remain at risk today. The lesson that spans East and West is that, given the creation of the right set of conditions, any region can host a wildfire. The transition in the twentieth

Table 2-1.
Significant U.S. Wildland Fires (Latter Half of the Twentieth Century)

Date	Name	Location	Acres	Significance
1949	Mann Gulch	Montana	4,339	13 Smokejumpers Killed
1967	Sundance	Idaho	56,000	Burned 50,000 acres in just nine hours
September 1970	Laguna	California	175,425	382 Structures Destroyed
July 1977	Sycamore	California	805	234 Structures Destroyed
November 1980	Panorama	California	23,600	325 Structures Destroyed
June 1990	Painted Cave	California	4,900	641 Structures Destroyed
June 1990	Dude Fire	Arizona	24,174	6 Lives Lost 63 homes destroyed
October 1991	Oakland Hills	California	1,500	25 Lives Lost and 2,900 Structures Destroyed
August 1992	Foothills Fire	Idaho	257,000	1 Life Lost
July 1994	South Canyon Fire	Colorado	1,856	14 Lives Lost
July 1994	Idaho City Complex	Idaho	154,000	1 Life Lost
June 1996	Millers Reach	Alaska	37,336	344 Structures Destroyed
1998	Volusia Complex	Florida	111,130	Thousands of people evacuated from several counties
August-November 1999	Big Bar Complex	California	140,947	Series of fires caused several evacuations during a 3½ month period
September-November 1999	Kirk Complex	California	86,700	Hundreds of people were evacuated by this complex of fires that burned for almost 3 months
May 2000	Cerro Grande	New Mexico	47,650	Originally a prescribed fire, 235 structures destroyed and Los Alamos National Laboratory damaged

Source: National Interagency Fire Center.

century was one in which the U.S. unwittingly replaced one set of hazardous conditions with another.

This is a selective list of some of the most serious wildland fires in the latter half of the twentieth century in the United States. Some were significant because of their size, others because of the value of the resources lost. Some small, but very intense, fires were important because of the loss of lives and property. There have been larger fires than some of those included on this list, but few or none with greater impact on lives and resources. The full list is available at http://www.nifc.gov/stats/historicalstats.html.

THE WAR ON FIRE

In the first decade of the twentieth century, about the time that the great wildfires of the upper Midwest were simmering down, President Theodore Roosevelt succeeded the assassinated William McKinley, and an important era began in American forestry. Gifford Pinchot, destined to become a legend in his field, succeeded in winning over both Roosevelt and Congress to the idea of placing the nation's extensive forest reserves under the aegis of the Bureau of Forestry, which he headed. This transfer of lands from the General Land Office, later renamed the Bureau of Land Management (BLM) under the United States Department of the Interior, was accomplished through the Transfer Act of 1905, legislation that essentially created the modern Forest Service under the United States Department of Agriculture (USDA). In large part, the logic of this agency being part of the USDA was that forest trees were viewed as a crop, thus a commodity. Therefore, Agriculture was a nicer fit than Interior, whose primary responsibility was the management of federal lands.

The effective result was that BLM became an agency holding those federal lands that no other agency wanted, while the Forest Service assumed control of many of the most wildfire-prone lands in the nation. (Many BLM grasslands, however, are also highly flammable.) With the steady decline during the nineteenth century of Native American influence over the western landscape, followed in the next century by a federal policy of aggressive wildfire suppression, biological fuels accumulated to unprecedented levels. The Forest Service, trying to establish its professionalism, elected to emphasize a scientific approach to understanding the problem but had no historical experience with managing such a vast domain. Inevitably, there came a season of drought, the arid mountains grew crisp and dry, and the scene exploded in a rash of wildfires in the summer of 1910. It was the sort of event that marks a wrenching of the consciousness of an institution, and it was followed by other fire seasons in the coming years. The Forest Service fought the fires, eventually gathering a work force of some 10,000 men that first year, with 1 million acres affected in Washington and Oregon, 3 million in Montana and Idaho, and other areas in California, South Dakota, and Nebraska. It was the beginning of a long, steady transformation of the Forest Service into a forest firefighting service.

In time, and it did not take long, an ideology grew around the massive campaigns to cope with the flames. The goal was simple: total suppression, meaning all forest fires should be extinguished as quickly as possible. With his usual flair for integrating cultural and technical considerations, Stephen Pyne (1982) notes the publication in 1910 of an essay by William James, the Harvard psychology professor, "On the Moral Equivalent of War." Invoking the concept of the "strenuous life" popularized by Roosevelt, it stated that the "martial type of character can be bred without war." James was a pacifist who nonetheless saw value in the hardy lifestyle produced by militarism and wished to turn it to other purposes for the public good, although in his eyes that included "human warfare against nature."

His essay, issued at the time of the massive 1910 wildfires in the West, constituted a call to arms that met the motivational needs of armies of wildland firefighters marching off to the nation's forests for decades thereafter to extinguish any fire that had started for any reason. The net result was an ideology of suppression and control that evolved with the technological means for waging war on fire. Pyne has categorized this evolution into four periods (Table 2-2). Over time the firefighting force in the wildlands, like the foresters themselves, became professional. At first composed of men simply in need of a temporary job, then, in the 1930s, of the billowing manpower supply of the Civilian Conservation Corps, it became a trained force, mostly of young men working seasonally until they wearied of the experience and moved on. Firefighting equipment evolved rapidly from rakes and shovels to water cannons to parachutes for smoke jumpers. The comparison to volunteer and draft-bred armies, and later to reservists, cannot be escaped, even if James had never written his essay. The nation had found the technical means to wage war on fire.

By the 1950s, even wartime propaganda took a dramatically effective new turn with the creation of Smokey Bear, the most effective public relations symbol of all time. Smokey actually followed a series of previous advertising campaigns beginning under the New Deal, enthusiastically supported by President Franklin Roosevelt, in an era when the nation, first because of the Depression, and later because of World War II, was willing to redefine the loss of thousands of acres of forest as unpatriotic and criminal waste. It was an attitude reinforced by perceptions that forest fires could be started within the U.S. as an act of sabotage. Late in the war, the Japanese attempt to penetrate the West Coast with fire balloons launched across the Pacific Ocean on the jet stream only served to strengthen such sentiments among nervous Forest Service personnel. The onset of the Cold War afterwards did little to relax such fears (Pyne 1982).

The problem, far clearer in retrospect than it was at the time, is that the policy of total suppression did not simply protect the forest in its natural state. It progressively altered its natural state. The policy of aggressively suppressing every forest fire, regardless of cause, failed to account adequately for the role of naturally caused wildfires—usually triggered by lightning strikes—in regulating the accumulation of burnable biomass (i.e., living or dead and decaying plant matter) in the forest. This allowed fuel loads to grow to levels far exceeding those of the past. The result was that,

Table 2-2.
Wildland Fire Protection: The U.S. Forest Service Experience

Date	Problem Fire	Policy	Fire Control Strategic Concept	Tactical Emphasis	Research
1910-1929	Frontier Fire	Economic Theory	Systematic fire protection	Administration	Fire as forestry Economics, planning, statistics of fire
1930-1949	Backcountry fire	10 A.M. Policy	Hour control	Manpower	
1950-1970	Mass fire	10 A.M. Policy	Conflagration control	Mechanization	Fire as physics Laboratory Field experimentation
1971-Present	Wilderness fire	Fire by prescription	Fuel modification	Prescribed (broadcast) fire	Fire as biology Natural laboratories Simulation experiments

Source: Pyne 1982.

when wildfires occurred, they feasted on far more dead foliage, under-story, and brush than ever before, making western fires in particular dangerously explosive conflagrations.

The Shift to Prescribed Fire

Lurking beneath the war on fire was a cultural undercurrent of détente with fire that had never completely died. In the South, especially, farmers and small landholders had long accommodated fire as a helpful tool in restraining the buildup of forest fuels, and the practice had long preceded them among Native Americans. With a more agrarian history in the region, old practices persisted well into the twentieth century despite criticisms from foresters, some of whom felt obliged to investigate why. At the same time, the South had its own impressive roster of fire statistics, which Pyne (1982) says have long dominated national statistics in number of fires and acreage burned. In one year early in the century, he notes, "it was reported that 105 percent of Florida burned." As elsewhere in the nation, Pyne traces the creation of many state forestry agencies, including Florida's, to a perceived need at the time to establish an adequate governmental mechanism for attacking forest fires.

Over time, the discovery that deliberate burning did serve some definable ecological purposes in reducing the forest fuel load allowed southern foresters to take the lead in helping to reshape official policies. Among these purposes, as wildlife refuge managers discovered, was the restoration and management of wildlife habitat. This is a practice with roots in both Native American and rural southern use of fire to enhance the feasibility of hunting, and in fact served the purposes of some hunting plantation managers in the South. Beginning in the late 1960s, with a series of experiments and technical conferences, the Tall Timbers Research Station in Tallahassee, Florida, became the center for advancing arguments on behalf of what has come to be known as "prescribed burns."

The term only hints at the shift of control that was effected in the planned use of fire from backwoods practitioners in the rural South to a cadre of professionally trained foresters. Foresters began to apply a growing scientific regime undergirding practices aimed at managing the impact of wildfires, rather than seeking to control them completely. Prescribed burns would limit the severity and spread of wildfires by denying them the volume and continuity of fuels that would otherwise sustain them. The methodology spread well beyond the South to acquire regional adaptations nationwide. Since the 1970s, the once-prevailing idea of fire as simply an enemy of both forests and mankind has given way to the much-nuanced notion of fire as a tool of ecological management. The idea of fighting wildfires uncompromisingly in order to preserve the forest in some primeval condition has yielded to the far more demanding realizations that humans have long influenced the shape of the forest and it is nearly impossible now to define that primeval condition. These new realizations suggest that managing the forest is not simply an option but a necessity. We are beyond the point where it is possible simply to "let nature take its course" because we have placed far too many assets in harm's way to be able in good conscience to refrain from mitigating the hazards we have created.

MODERN DEVELOPMENT OF WUI

Beginning in the 1950s, abetted by the combined growth of suburban development and automobile dependency, a new phenomenon emerged on the stage of American land-use development. Middle-class and affluent homeowners, initially in California, then elsewhere, moved into subdivisions built in wildfire-prone hills and woodlands at the urban fringe.

We are beyond the point where it is possible simply to "let nature take its course" because we have placed far too many assets in harm's way to be able in good conscience to refrain from mitigating the hazards we have created.

People have long lived in the forest. In the South, however, it was largely the domain of small-scale farmers. In the Rocky Mountain West, a relatively modest population of settlers attracted by agriculture and mining opportunities was scattered across the landscape. None of them expected or demanded any amenities beyond what they could build for themselves. When fires occurred, their numbers were few, and they often had their own voluntary means of response. The large numbers of human casualties in historical fires had been a result of record-breaking conflagrations sweeping through midwestern logging towns when Minnesota was still the frontier. By the 1920s, that era was largely over.

The movement of middle-class and upper-middle-class homeowners into the woods in large, preplanned subdivisions in California, however, was different. Such developments had occurred as early as the 1920s, in places like the East Bay Hills in Oakland and Berkeley. A major fire in 1923 destroyed 584 structures in Berkeley, an ominous foreshadowing of 14 more that followed until the infamous October 1991 Tunnel Fire that consumed 2,900 structures and killed 25 people (Schwab et al. 1998).

By the 1950s, California was undergoing a development boom that soon made it not only the most populous state in the nation, but also propelled it along a growth trajectory with which no other state could compete. Growth around Los Angeles, like the Bay Area, spread into the hills, particularly newly fashionable suburbs like Malibu. It was the beginning of what sociologists more recently have labeled "amenity migration," the movement toward rural (or formerly rural) areas, allowing residents to feel they are in closer contact with nature. Pyne (1982) notes, where most modern suburbs are relatively fireproof because mowed lawns and paved streets do little to convey fire toward homes, the new, often more exclusive, developments sought to incorporate brush and forest as part of their natural aesthetics at the same time they incorporated wood shingles into their structures. The result not only perpetuates the natural cycle of fire that has always affected the area, but exacerbates it by injecting new fuels—the homes and structures themselves—into the mix, while reinforcing the urgency of suppressing fires anywhere within the vicinity.

Fire experts warned early on that this was a recipe for calamity. In Southern California, local fire agencies sought an investigation by the National Fire Protection Association (NFPA). NFPA responded with a conflagration warning in 1958, but residential expansion into the Santa Monica Mountains and other forests and foothills continued apace (Pyne 1982). Fire followed fire, in Bel Air and Brentwood, in the Hollywood Hills, in the chaparral country above San Diego, and in San Bernardino County.

It was the beginning of what sociologists more recently have labeled "amenity migration," the movement toward rural (or formerly rural) areas, allowing residents to feel they are in closer contact with nature.

Burned-out homesites still dotted the hillsides of Oakland, California, even three years after the 1991 wildfire.

Jim Schwab

The desire to live in the hills and the woods has never been strictly a California phenomenon. The media focus on California is largely a function of numbers. As noted in Chapter 1, although it took longer to materialize, development in Florida is steadily pushing inland from the coasts, where some 80 percent of the population has traditionally lived. Consequently, Florida's encounters with wildfire hazards, and the need to mitigate them, have grown. Colorado, Utah, Idaho, Nevada, Arizona, New Mexico, Oregon, and Washington all are experiencing rapid growth. All are acquiring serious problems with WUI development, including outlying vacation and resort homes in resort communities and rural areas. Other parts of the country are affected as well. Under drought conditions, even eastern and northern states become exposed to WUI problems, as did New York when the Pine Barrens on Long Island went up in flames in 1995.

One upshot of these developments is that the nation needs and is getting a new focus in its data-gathering efforts related to wildfires. Historically, news often centered on the sheer number of acres on fire. Until recently, however, that figure has not often varied a great deal from year to year. Most of those acres are typically in large, relatively uninhabited areas on federal lands. Many of those federal lands, however, are checkered with inholdings of private landowners. What matters more in the era of WUI is the defense of developed residential areas, which increases the costs and complexity of fire suppression. Federal expenditures have risen notably in the last 10 years (Table 2-3). Those outlays, which have continued to escalate since 2000, were the impetus for both the National Fire Plan and the federally funded National Academy of Public Administration (NAPA) studies on controlling the cost of suppressing wildfires (NAPA 2002a).

Among the developing issues accompanying the growth of WUI development is that neither wildland nor local firefighters are ideally trained for the task. Many rural volunteer fire districts are supported only by minimal property taxes and lack the capacity to deal with large-scale urban development in unincorporated areas. The state of California, notes Colorado State Forest Service planner Nan Johnson (2004), is the only

Table 2-3.
Fire Suppression Costs for Federal Agencies (in millions of $)

Year	Bureau of Land Management	Bureau of Indian Affairs	Fish and Wildlife Service	National Park Service	USDA Forest Service	Totals
1994	98.417	49.202	3.281	16.362	678.000	845.262
1995	56.600	36.219	1.675	21.256	224.300	340.050
1996	98.854	40.779	—	19.832	521.700	679.168
1997	62.470	30.916	—	6.844	155.768	256.000
1998	63.177	27.366	3.800	19.183	215.000	328.526
1999	85.724	42.183	4.500	30.061	361.000	523.468
2000	180.567	93.042	9.417	53.341	1,026.000	1,362.367
2001	192.115	63.200	7.160	48.092	607.233	917.800
2002	204.666	109.035	15.245	66.094	1,266.274	1,661.314
2003	151.894	96.633	9.554	44.557	1,023.500	1,326.138

Source: National Interagency Fire Center.

exception, with the California Department of Forestry paying for staff in rural areas. Wildland firefighters traditionally have engaged in fighting forest fires with little training and experience in structural firefighting; that is, the protection of individual structures. In WUI, they concentrate on structure protection, which is the defense of the building from the outside against an advancing forest fire. Urban firefighters, on the other hand, are largely oriented to structural firefighting, which involves extinguishing fires within the interior of a building, and rescuing occupants trapped inside. It is not surprising then that costs of suppression begin to rise when each force is pressed more often to respond to situations for which it is not well trained.

Ron Montague (2004a and b), vice-president of Firewise 2000, Inc., a Murrieta, California, consulting firm, raises an issue of long-term planning that portends additional firefighting costs in the future: the lack of integration of fire concerns into other types of land management planning, such as the development of watershed plans, multispecies habitat conservation plans, and open space preservation. This lack of integration of plans represents in each case a lost opportunity for considering a more holistic, sustainable development pattern for the community or region, even more so when neighboring jurisdictions fail to coordinate such plans among themselves because wildfires do not respect political boundaries. The upshot will be even more need, Montague says, for "urban and volunteer fire departments to protect structures and sensitive habitat without wildland fire equipment and training."

It is also worth noting that the 2000 Cerro Grande fire in Los Alamos introduced another dilemma into the equation. Prescribed burns, although they have gained acceptance as a forest management tool among professionals, remain controversial with many segments of the public. Some people do not like the smoke and complain of the seemingly deliberate generation of air pollution, not necessarily accounting for the air-quality impact of a truly catastrophic fire in the future if nothing is done. Some simply do not understand the point of it at all, perhaps regarding it as reckless. It takes but one incident of a prescribed burn raging out of control to arouse latent suspicions that the professionals do not fully understand what they are doing. Cerro Grande helped fuel that suspicion when a prescribed burn spread to devour hundreds of homes and damage part of Los Alamos National Laboratory. The result in part was a series of recriminations concerning the whole program. In the end, it did not stifle or terminate prescribed burns, but it was a reminder that such programs depend on a sometimes thin veneer of public trust (NIFC 2000). Lost in the debate, however, were questions about what made so many homes and the nuclear laboratory facilities in Los Alamos so vulnerable, a question that remains pressing because the same fire could have had any number of other origins. For instance, residential development could have steered clear of areas close to the base of a forested mountain through effective growth management tied to good hazard mapping (Johnson 2000).

Prescribed burns are hardly the only controversial element in the quiver of mitigation options available to planners, foresters, and other professionals. It is no secret that there is not always an abundance of trust between environmentalists, federal land agencies, and local communities over issues like forest thinning and timber harvests. This distrust can be a serious obstacle to the reduction of wildfire hazards and better development policies in hazardous areas. It is vital communities and their officials better comprehend forest health conditions, wildland fire functions, and the implications these facts have both for community design in the interface and for wildfire mitigation programs, such as prescribed burns and other fuel reduction measures.

Prescribed burns, although they have gained acceptance as a forest management tool among professionals, remain controversial with many segments of the public.

CHAPTER 3

The Science of Wildfires

"The Science of Wildfires" is almost certainly not listed on the curriculum of any planning schools. Although it may fit into courses on natural hazards taught in some planning schools, for the vast majority of planners it is new subject matter. Moreover, much of what matters with relation to planning for the wildland-urban interface (WUI) is the result of relatively recent research. Before moving to the big issues in planning for wildfires, it is worthwhile to provide an overview of what planners need to know about how wildfires behave. This knowledge has important implications for both site planning and building design in areas with wildfire hazards.

THE ECOLOGIGAL ROLE OF FIRE

The ignitions that spark wildfires, like the weather conditions that foster them, are notoriously unpredictable. The mere fact the right conditions exist for their occurrence does not produce a certainty they will occur. There is a great deal of room in ecological science for improvements in our knowledge of just how fire influences the environment. Despite this, we have already learned a great deal in recent decades to help us shape better public policy. The goal of this chapter is to provide an overview for planners of the basic scientific principles of wildfire, which involve fuel, weather, and topography.

"The land is a quilt of burnable biomasses," Stephen J. Pyne (2001) has written, "some patches vast, some tiny, much of that organic matter available for burning, some not." Pyne, a professor of history at Arizona State University and the author of an entire series of books called "Cycle of Fire," has become the leading authority on the history of fire around the world. He stresses the fitful nature of both fire and biological adaptation to it, lest we assume we know more about evolutionary cause and effect than may be the case. He observes this quilt, wildly variable from one region of the world to the next, which makes fire possible through a necessary tension between wet and dry, living and dead biomass. Moisture is essential for plant growth. Without it, we have not even a desert but a dead planet. With too much of it, nothing will burn because too much thermal energy is consumed in vaporizing the water to permit ignition. In order for natural fire to thrive, plants need enough water to grow, but enough dryness to catch fire and burn. In many parts of the world, conditions alternate between rainy and dry seasons, in the short term, and between periods of prolonged wetness and prolonged drought over much longer periods.

Plants respond to natural fire regimes as part of their environment, but the evolutionary adaptations vary, and the variations are far too complex to be enumerated here. According to the Fire Sciences Lab, an arm of the Rocky Mountain Research Station in Missoula, Montana, "A natural fire regime is a general classification of the role fire would play across a landscape in the absence of modern human mechanic intervention, but including the influence of aboriginal burning." These regimes fall into five categories varying from great frequency (0–35 years) and low severity to

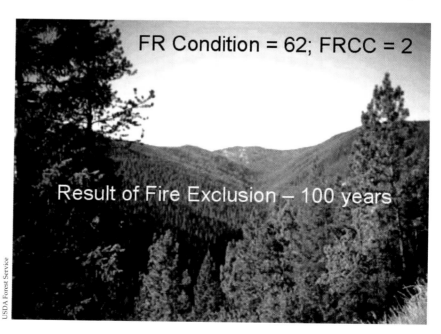

The U.S. Forest Service classifies fire regimes according to condition class, based on frequency and severity of wildfires. This photo from the Fire Regime Condition Class Web site (frcc.gov) illustrates the forest density resulting from a century of fire suppression policies.

USDA Forest Service

infrequent intervals (200+ years) and high severity. A fire regime condition class, in turn, is "a classification of the amount of departure from the natural regime." (The details of this classification system can be found at www.frcc.gov and www.fire.org.) It is worth noting that some basic variations exist among plants. Whelan (1995) describes the differences between sprouters and obligate seeders, the latter being plants that depend on fire for germination. Many Native Americans and others have fostered grasslands at the expense of forest growth by using fire to elicit such growth. In turn, the availability of one type of forage versus another influences the viability of specific animal populations that feed on them, which may in turn affect populations of their predators.

There are also important differences in the flammability of various types of vegetation. Some trees, like palmetto, piñon pine, and eucalyptus, have oily resins that easily intensify wildfires, while other plants are relatively resistant to fire. In Florida, for instance, the latter group includes dogwood, native oak trees, native ferns, and azaleas (Florida DCA and Florida DACS 2004). In the Southwest, the juniper burns extremely hot. Aspen, on the other hand, drops its leaves in fire and is a recommended type of vegetation. For planning purposes, such as drafting an effective landscaping code for fire-prone areas, this type of information is essential in crafting defensible space around homes and entire subdivisions. However, knowing what works will depend on understanding how such plants function in the local environment. Simply transferring landscaping practices from one region to another can produce serious adverse results. Even recommended plants placed in poorly adapted sites can have adverse consequences. Fortunately for planners, landscape architects, developers, and many state and university forestry departments, driven by the widespread search for answers to this problem, have produced lists of regionally or locally appropriate vegetation for wildfire mitigation purposes.

WHAT IS NATURAL?

Underlying these issues in wildfire ecology is a more vexing, larger question. Just what is the natural level of fire in any particular regional environment? For that matter, what is a "natural forest," and what were the pre-settlement conditions of our forests? It is not easy to separate the influence of human activity from the biological and even paleontological records available to us. Examinations of scar patterns in old growth trees, for instance, may tell us the frequency of fires but not their origins. We know lightning strikes currently make up only a small portion of the overall total of ignitions, but that does not tell us how extensively such fires burned before humans became a factor. In other words, the sheer extent of the human presence around the world and the sheer extent of human use and/ or suppression of fire even in pre-modern societies make it extremely difficult to identify the impact of those wildfires not caused by humans. In any event, given the scope of development in the U.S. and other industrial societies, attempting to return to any assumed natural fire regime is simply not possible.

What is possible is to attempt to manage fire to achieve healthy ecosystems surrounding and within our communities. The essential point about fire's role in the environment is that, like rain, wind, and some flooding, it serves a vital function within the environment, maintaining an ecological balance over time. The belief that wildland fire can and must always be suppressed serves in the long run only to exacerbate the severity of fires when they finally occur.

It is problematic, therefore, to talk about natural fire cycles in an age when so many fires originate from human activities. As statistics in Chapter 1

Underlying these issues in wildfire ecology is a more vexing, larger question. Just what is the natural level of fire in any particular regional environment?

show, today truly natural sources of ignition—primarily lightning (though volcanoes and similar geological phenomena can also ignite wildfires)—are no longer the dominant cause of wildfires. Even in Alaska, seemingly remote but with the longest human presence in the Western Hemisphere, modern fire is inextricably bound to human influences (Pyne 1982).

The effects of any individual fire do not depend on whether the origin is natural or human. Once a fire starts, so far as both plants and animals are affected, fire is fire. However, anthropogenic causes do alter the frequency, intensity, and spread of fires in an area. Moreover, individual fires are highly variable in their effects because ecological systems react differently to variations in intensity of fire, the speed of its advance through the environment, and other factors. There is a big difference, in other words, between the immediate impact on a local environment of any single fire and the long-term impact of an entire fire regime over extended periods of time (Whelan 1995).

THE PHYSICS OF WILDFIRES

The physical characteristics of fire are fairly basic. Fire is a chemical transformation that depends entirely on three necessary ingredients: heat, fuel, and oxygen. Remove any one of them, and combustion cannot occur. For example, water is used to extinguish fire because increasing the moisture of the fuel increases the amount of heat required to dry the fuel sufficiently to maintain its flammability, thus acting as a counteragent to the heat generated by the fire itself. Apply enough water, and the fire cannot sustain itself. Likewise, smothering a fire, for example, by covering it with a blanket, cuts off the oxygen needed for combustion, even though the blanket itself is a somewhat flammable substance. (However, smoldering fires can lurk beneath snow, in duff, or in old mine shafts or coal seams, with just enough oxygen to persist for extended periods—in underground environments, sometimes for years.) In a big enough fire, such a strategy will result only in burning the blanket. Chemical agents that smother the fire by blocking access to oxygen are then required instead. The effectiveness of smothering depends on the relative balance and supply of the three ingredients. Fuel consists basically of carbohydrates or hydrocarbons that will react with the oxygen and heat to promote combustion. Removing such substances from the path of a fire thus becomes another strategy in fire fighting.

It is important to distinguish between what ignites a fire and what sustains it. Once started, a fire may often overcome obstacles to its spread that would have been strong enough to prevent its initial outbreak. The primary obstacle of consequence is the presence of moisture in fuel sources.

There is a big difference, in other words, between the immediate impact on a local environment of any single fire and the long-term impact of an entire fire regime over extended periods of time.

Figure 3-1. Fire Triangle Credit: Florida DCA and Florida DACS

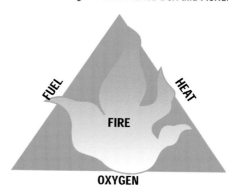

Source: Florida DCA and Florida DACS 2004.

A higher level of energy, in the form of heat, is required to ignite moist fuels than to burn them once ignition has taken place, largely because the heat generated by the advancing fire serves to vaporize moisture in the fuels that lie in its path before the flames actually consume them. Fires advance from being exothermic, meaning they need a heat source to proceed, to endothermic, meaning the heat generated by the fire itself makes it self-sustaining (Whelan 1995).

As a result, a roaring fire has far more potential to burn even moist fuel, such as a decaying leaf pile, than a lightning strike has of igniting it in the first place. What fuel moisture will do, however, is retard the spread of the fire by making it expend more heat (and thus take more time) to burn wet fuels than dry fuels. Weather, however, can also be a potent factor in removing moisture from flammable biomass, just as it adds such moisture through precipitation. A prolonged drought combined with high temperatures dries out dead and dying biomass, such as leaves, brown grass, and pine needles, increasing the likelihood of ignition. Montague (2004a) notes that "hot dry winds accelerate the transpiration process, and the plant is unable to replenish with groundwater. . . . [Some] winds can dry out vegetation very rapidly, especially on exposed north or east slopes known

Florida Division of Forestry

Surface Fire

Florida Department of Community Affairs

Crown Fire

Florida Department of Community Affairs

Ground Fire

for their more moist fuel conditions." Once ignition has taken place, the fuel itself sustains the fire's energy until the supply is exhausted. It becomes apparent with this description why human sources of ignition easily multiply the frequency of fires over purely natural sources. Lightning often is accompanied by rain in a thunderstorm, making many natural fires somewhat self-limiting, although lightning can accompany the dry side of a thunderstorm cell. An exception is a region like the American Southwest, where a common pattern of dry lightning strikes is a more volatile generator of natural wildfires.

Suppression Strategies

Once a wildfire is underway, strategies to contain or suppress it necessarily revolve around the three ingredients cited earlier—heat, fuel, and oxygen. Unlike urban firefighters, whose efforts are focused on suppressing structural fires, wildland firefighters must develop strategies in concert with what nature offers them in order to be maximally effective and to preserve their own safety. Weather conditions, topography, and local vegetation become factors in coping with an advancing wildfire. Having no ability to affect the topography or weather, suppression efforts try to modify the vegetation or fuels to bring a fire under control. Otherwise, suppression efforts must await changes in weather conditions, such as rain, snow, or a lapse in winds.

Weather conditions, topography, and local vegetation become factors in coping with an advancing wildfire.

Weather forecasts matter because changes in temperature, wind direction (pushing flames forward or back), and precipitation all may play a role in making the fight against a wildfire easier or more difficult. These factors all play some role in either adding to or reducing the heat that sustains the fire.

Artificial heat reduction is most typically achieved by dousing a fire with water, forcing the fire to expend more energy to consume the fuel in its path. The effectiveness of this strategy is far greater in smaller urban fires than in large wildland fires because of the differences in scale involved. Nonetheless, where appropriate steps have been taken beforehand to mitigate fire vulnerabilities around structures in the interface, fire departments can and do use massive spraying and aerial drops of fire retardants effectively to protect individual homes or whole subdivisions.

Fuel deprivation is the strategy behind fuel breaks, which are strips of land in which fuels have been treated in some way in order to interrupt the progress of a fire, assuming that the advancing flames cannot jump over the barrier. This can be done in various ways, for instance, in oak wood-lands by treating the understory and removing lower branches to prevent a fire from climbing into the tree canopy. Removing dead material from shrubs and bushes can also be effective. Montague (2004a) indicates three goals of a fuel break:

- Provide enhancements contributing to wildland fire control

- Bring the fire to ground level and provide adequate separation of ladder fuels to prevent crown fires

- Slow, retard, or direct the spread of the fire

The fuel break may be permanent (such as the tightly mowed grass often seen along utility right-of-way corridors) or improvised in the course of fighting a particular wildfire. The latter strategy explains the many scenes from old wildfire photos of workers carrying shovels and axes into the woods. In more recent times, this highly labor-intensive strategy has been replaced with more mechanized attacks on the problem. Using deliberate backfires to remove fuel in advance of the fire, leaving only burned veg-etation behind for the wildfire itself, is another way of starving it of fuel along its anticipated path.

Fuel breaks are not always a perfect strategy. Montague (2004a) notes fuel breaks are often ineffective against the head of a fire but relatively successful along its flanks. In a larger fire, flying embers can be distributed as much as 1.5 miles by the resulting convection and prevailing winds. They can then ignite a new fuel source downwind, thus leapfrogging the constructed fuel break. For instance, Cohen (1999) found in the 1991 fires in Spokane, Washington, and elsewhere that homes with flammable roofs caught fire from firebrands even in the absence of the surrounding vegeta-tion burning. Nonetheless, fuel breaks can improve the odds of halting the fire's advance. They are especially effective for ground-level fires, where the chance of flying embers is greatly reduced, and less effective for crown fires, which spread across treetops within a forest.

The one thing nearly impossible in a wildfire setting is denying oxygen to the advancing fire. This strategy works well enough in many urban struc-tural fires, where such containment is largely a technical challenge, but to accomplish it in an outdoor setting, particularly with a fire that may be consuming hundreds, or even thousands, of acres of vegetation is some-thing rarely seen. About the only situation in which it has ever been effectively used is in using blankets and similar devices to stifle smaller grassland fires. One part of American lore, in fact, consists of frontier stories where pioneers used such tactics, as in the tales of Mari Sandoz (1992) from the Nebraska Sandhills at the end of the nineteenth century.

Just as there are necessary ingredients to ignite or sustain a fire, there are certain factors that influence its direction and spread.

Factors Influencing Wildfire Spread

Just as there are necessary ingredients to ignite or sustain a fire, there are certain factors that influence its direction and spread, and they vary sig-nificantly with the local landscape, making mapping of wildfire hazards and a knowledge of the local terrain essential for planners and firefighters alike. These are not static dimensions, however, and should not be mapped as such. Seasonal weather patterns can alter the level of hazard within the same area over time, a fact that is critical in developing strategies for fight-ing a fire once it is underway. Tracking anticipated weather patterns, including wind direction, temperatures, and precipitation, is also critical in planning the use of prescribed fires, as the tragic example of the Cerro Grande fire in Los Alamos, New Mexico, makes clear (NIFC 2000).

Whelan (1995) outlines three essential factors in the spread of wildfires:

- fuel continuity;

- topography; and

- plant communities.

Fuel continuity has both natural and artificial dimensions, the latter noted above in the discussion of suppression strategies. Natural breaks in fuel continuity can consist of previously burned areas that have not yet recovered sufficiently to rebuild a supply of biomass to feed the fire (part of the strategy behind prescribed fires). A sizeable patch of grasslands can greatly reduce the available biomass in the path of a fire as compared to a stretch of shrubby vegetation or trees. The height of grasses, however, can make a significant difference in the amount of fuel available. Grazing by ruminant livestock can actually serve as an effective nonmechanical means of reducing such growth (FEMA 2004). Goats are most effective in brush areas, while cattle, horses, and llamas are more effective in grass (Montague 2004a).

Fuel continuity is vertical as well as horizontal. Fires can move upwards in forests only if there is sufficient easily burnable fuel stretching up the sides of trees, or accumulated on the forest floor, to allow the fire to reach the upper leaves and branches. This vegetation is known as ladder fuels because it allows the flames to advance up the tree trunks, which are generally more resistant to burning. Taller trees whose limbs are well above the forest floor therefore pose more of an obstacle to the vertical advance of the fire than trees whose lower limbs can be reached by flames advancing upwards. When a wildfire succeeds in climbing the forest understory to set ablaze the upper foliage of the trees, the result is a crown fire, an extremely dangerous situation in which flames, often driven by winds whose force may be exacerbated by convection from the heat of the fire itself, can leap across the tops of the forest canopy, allowing the winds to carry burning embers aloft to destinations a mile or more downwind. As fuel, in the form of dead biomass, accumulates in the forest, the conditions and probabilities for crown fires improve.

Topography includes all those natural features of the landscape that may facilitate or interrupt the advance of the fire. Bodies of water, for example, can serve this purpose if sufficiently wide. Small creeks, in most cases, will not present an effective barrier if bordered by more highly flammable vegetation. Whelan (1995) notes that red pine forests in Minnesota are now found only on island habitats in Lake Duparquet, unreachable by the mainland fires that have consumed other such forests. One factor of special significance in a peninsular state like Florida is the "cape effect," (Figure 3-2) in which incoming breezes advance landward from all sides due to the coastal convection currents. This produces a convergence of wind on land that experiences frequent thunderstorms, with the possibility of intensifying any fire that erupts.

Lakes and rivers may be important factors in the spread of wildfires in flatland forests in states like Minnesota and Florida, but they are much less significant in the arid West. On the other hand, the presence of canyons and mountains figures greatly there. These topographical features influence wind movement, often intensifying wind velocity or erratic wind patterns in narrow drainages, driving fires up the sides of hills and allowing flames to leap to new fuel sources in ways not possible on level ground. Fire most often moves faster uphill, with longer flames, than on level ground or when moving downhill. This rapid movement preheats the fuel above the flames by convection, adding to its flammability. Figure 3-3 provides some examples of the difference in fire behavior produced by both wind and slope.

Figure 3-2. The Cape Effect.

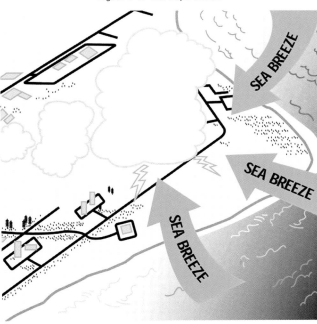

Source: Florida DCA and Florida DACS.

Figure 3-3. Differences in Fire Behavior Caused by Wind and Slope

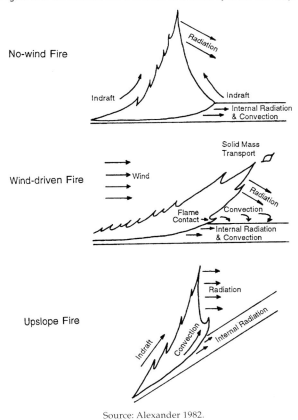

The similar influences of wind and topography on fire behavior are illustrated in these fire profiles. Both slope and wind bring the flames nearer the adjacent, unburnt fuel, so enhancing the pre-heating and increasing the rate of spread.

Source: Alexander 1982.

Slope is an important consideration in fire hazard rating precisely because of the way it influences fire behavior, such as extending flame lengths. This happens in large part because of the way in which wind currents traverse hillsides, pushing flames forward and making homes at the crest of a hill

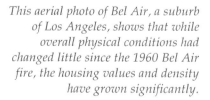

This aerial photo of Bel Air, a suburb of Los Angeles, shows that while overall physical conditions had changed little since the 1960 Bel Air fire, the housing values and density have grown significantly.

more vulnerable than those downhill from a wildfire. One exception, according to Montague (2004a), is that strong winds (chinooks, foehn, or Santa Ana) can drive fires in a way that overwhelms the topographic impacts. These winds were particularly important in Southern California's 2003 firestorm. Any vegetation on slopes, including stands of trees growing along the side of the hill, can act very effectively as ladder fuels leading straight into the homes or other structures above them.

Homeowners who add wooden decks overlooking the hillside in such landscapes are then escalating their own hazard level. Slope has become a major factor in hazard rating systems. The National Fire Protection Agency (NFPA) 1144 publication, a national standard discussed in Chapter 4, defines slope as the most significant factor (see Table 3-1).

Aspect, or the directional orientation of a structure, can also play a role in the frequency of fires threatening the area around it. North-facing slopes in the northern hemisphere receive less sunlight than those facing south, with the result that greater moisture remains on the ground in the form of dew, making potential fuels wetter and harder to burn than those receiving more direct sunlight. There can also be noticeable differences in temperature between two sides of a mountain for the same reason. Average daily temperature affects dryness and ambient heat, both of which are critical factors in the ignition of wildfires. Orientation is thus another valid factor for use in hazard severity ratings.

Finally, **plant communities** differ in their flammability. As noted earlier, certain species with oily resins are far more ignitable than those that lack such characteristics. Not only will this influence the spread of the fire within natural forests, but it also becomes a vital element in planning fire-resistant landscapes around the built environment. Whelan (1995) also notes that plants differ in their capacity to generate firebrands that can become wind-borne, as described above.

Whole regional ecosystems can also vary both in their flammability and in their amenability to fuel treatments, such as prescribed burns. For instance, the chaparral landscape of parts of coastal Southern California is particularly susceptible to wildfire, and questions have been raised in recent research about whether prescribed burns are capable of making any difference in the level of hazard or may even make it worse (Keeley 2002). While this may raise serious questions about the suitability of such an

Table 3-1.
Wildland Fire Hazard Severity Classification Analysis by Fuel Type, Slope, and Building Material

NFDRS Fuel Models	FBO Fuel Models	Slope Percent[1]			Building Material Combustibility[2]
		0–20%	21–0%	41+%	
H, R	8 Grass	L	L	M	L or M or H
U, P, E	9 Timber	L	L	M	L or M or H
K	11 Slash	L	M	H	L or M or H
A, L, S	1 Grass	L	M	H	L or M or H
D	7 Shrub	L	M	H	L or M or H
N	3 Grass	M	M	H	L or M or H
G	10 Timber	M	M	H	L or M or H
F	5 Shrub	M	M	H	L or M or H
C, T	2 Grass	M	M	H	L or M or H
F, Q	6 Shrub	M	H	H	L or M or H
J	12 Slash	M	H	H	L or M or H
I	13 Slash	M	H	H	L or M or H
B, O	4 Shrub	H	H	H	L or M or H

[1] Wildland fire hazard ratings are as follows: L = low; M = moderate; or H = high.
[2] Building material combustibility ratings are as follows:
L = Low (Class A roof; noncombustible siding and deck).
M = Moderate (Class B roof; noncombustible siding and deck).
H = High (Class C or nonrated roof; combustible siding and deck).
Source: NFPA 2002.

ecosystem to host any significant amount of development, Montague (2004a) says chaparral flammability is "directly related to fuel moisture conditions and age class" of the vegetation. The older the chaparral, the greater the buildup of fine dead fuels. Thus, prescribed burns could be used selectively to vary the age class of the vegetation and remove dead fuels.

Ratings of the comparative flammability and drought tolerance of various types of vegetation are available from many cooperative extension services and state forestry agencies. Because of the regionalized nature of most flora, state-level data are generally the most useful for determining effective landscaping strategies in a local area. Virginia Tech's Cooperative Extension has one such guide to assist with Firewise landscaping. In general, evergreen trees and shrubs have much higher flammability ratings than most deciduous trees, but resinous trees of any type are by nature highly flammable because the oils ignite easily (Virginia Firewise Landscaping Task Force 1998). Pine needles add to the problem because they dry out much faster than leaves. Chaparral is another highly flammable type of vegetation whose dangers are difficult to mitigate.

Density of vegetation is the driving issue behind forest thinning strategies. Greater spacing reduces the likelihood of flames leaping from one tree to another, and reduces the overall fuel load. With a wildfire in progress, however, this will usually serve mostly to reduce the intensity of the fire rather than to slow its progress entirely.

IMPLICATIONS FOR THE BUILT ENVIRONMENT
The most significant issues facing planners with regard to wildfire hazards are how these principles and data relate to sound design of any new

construction in areas containing such hazards, as well as the best strategies for mitigating the hazards in areas already built. The next two chapters will deal more directly with the experiences of various communities in wrestling with these questions. This chapter will conclude with an overview of how the physics of wildfires affect housing and other structures in the WUI.

This discussion must start by emphasizing that homes on sloped sites pose significantly greater challenges that make the proper maintenance of defensible space around them even more crucial than for other homes in the WUI. As noted above, such sites exacerbate the vulnerability of the homes built on them. It must be assumed that flame lengths may be longer and that stricter measures must be undertaken to limit the access of fire into openings extending beneath or into the home, as well as limiting those types of vegetation that could serve as ladder fuels to reach the home from an upwardly approaching fire. The Firewise zones described below must all be expanded as slope increases. Chapter 4 discusses how some local ordinances handle slope as a factor in calculating defensible space.

One critical factor related to slope nonetheless introduces an issue for subdivision planning in all wildland communities: access. In order to effectively evacuate residents and to provide rapid access for firefighters, multiple routes into and out of the subdivision are necessary. On flat land, such access may be relatively easy to provide. In rugged terrain, however, it can become so problematic as to raise questions about the fundamental wisdom of a development proposal if such access cannot be provided. Without adequate access and evacuation routes, the potential exists for homes to become death traps.

The most important question in protecting homes in the WUI is how structures are ignited by wildfires. Structures are ignited in one of three ways:

One critical factor related to slope nonetheless introduces an issue for subdivision planning in all wildland communities: access.

- *Radiation.* Flames radiate heat, and that heat can raise the temperature of structures within the proximity of their flame lengths. However, these distances are limited, even for large crown fires, to a maximum of 40 meters, or about 135 feet. In most cases, however, especially for ground-level fires, those radiation distances may be substantially less (Cohen 1999). Basically, homes are at risk of ignition from radiation when it elevates the temperature of flammable materials to their ignition level, somewhere between 583 and 727 degrees Fahrenheit (Florida DCA and Florida DACS 2004).

This subdivision has only one access route. Residents could be trapped if a wildfire closed off the entry road.

USDA Forest Service

- *Convection.* This occurs when flames make direct contact with the structure. Convection is a significant factor when fuels are available in close proximity to a house or structure, for example, wood piles, shrubbery, or an accumulation of dead leaves, grass, pine needles, etc.

- *Firebrands.* Winds can carry burning embers aloft, sometimes up to a mile or more, depending on weather and topography. The formation of embers depends both on the type of vegetation burning in the wildfire and on the type of fire, with crown fires posing greater dangers. Firebrands are most dangerous when they have the opportunity to land on flammable roofs, for example wood shakes, or can be sucked into homes through openings in eaves or soffits, or beneath wooden decking, borne inward by air currents. They can also ignite nearby vegetation, creating the opportunity for igniting the home through the resulting convection.

The foregoing delineation of the causes of home ignition points to some logical conclusions about strategies for protecting structures in the WUI. The central concept is that of defensible space (see Figure 3-5). This involves creating a zone around the structure that consists of an adequate arrangement of major sources of fuel to minimize the chances of ignition and to increase the odds for the home's survival without firefighting intervention. For this reason, it is important to understand the related concept of the home ignition zone (HIZ), defined as that area around a home, about 30 feet, which determines the potential for ignition in the event of a wildfire (Cohen, Johnson, and Walther 2001). All of the factors discussed thus far play into the ignition potential of the HIZ:

Figure 3-4. Radiation, Convection, and Firebrands are Sources of Ignition of Structures in the Wildland-Urban Interface.

Source: Florida DCA and Florida DACS 2004.

Figure 3-5. Sloped Sites with and without Defensible Space.

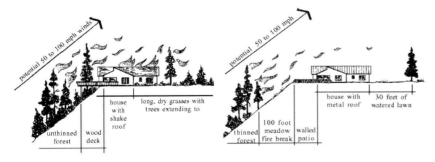

House *without* defensible space
- House at crest of hill at risk
- Shrubs below deck and tree through deck add to fire danger.
- Shake roof burns easily.

House *with* defensible space
- House set back from crest is sheltered.
- Stone walls deflect fire.
- Fire-proof roof protects house from embers
- Enclosed eaves reduce fires risk.
- Greatest clearing downhill from house.

Source: Idaho Cooperative Extension.

- The *flammability* of materials within the HIZ, such as roofs, decks, and other exterior features of the home; living or dead vegetation, such as trees, grass, and shrubs; and other flammable substances, such as wood piles and petroleum-derived fuels.

- Influences on *fire behavior*, such as slope and exterior design features including overhanging eaves or decks, which can allow flames to be drawn into the house. One way to minimize such dangers is to place tight wire mesh over any openings in eaves, soffits, and chimneys. (The Firewise Web site, www.firewise.org, offers a variety of publications and videos detailing how this can best be done.)

The Firewise Landscaping Checklist divides the area surrounding an interface home into four zones. Zone 1 is a 30-foot space immediately surrounding the structure, with each subsequent zone extending further out to progressively greater diameters, depending on conditions, such as fuel type and slope (see sidebar).

Throughout the property, homeowners need to make an effort to remove debris such as leaves, pine needles, and grass cuttings. Chapter 4 contains more detail on specific regulations and guidelines, which should be adapted to their specific geographic settings.

Rehm et al. (2002), in a study of wildfire spread for the National Institute of Standards and Technology (NIST) observe that Pyne, Andrew, and Laven (1996) have categorized fuel types according to their fuel load and energy characteristics, as shown in Table 3-2. One can easily see why logging slash ignited such powerful fires in the nineteenth century, as noted in Chapter 2. But it also becomes clear that there are significant differences in the characteristics of chaparral, a highly flammable plant type, and short grasses; it is also an argument for not allowing grass to remain untended in undeveloped lots in the interface.

Once the area surrounding the home has been addressed in order to reduce opportunities for ignition or convection, the flammability of the home itself must also be considered. Rehm, et al. (2002) state that houses, because of the density of their materials, typically provide several times the fuel loading of the surrounding forest. This heavy fuel loading, in fact, facilitates rapid fire spread in a dense subdivision that is poorly designed

FIREWISE LANDSCAPING

Zone 1. This well-irrigated area encircles the structure for at least 30' on all sides, providing space for fire-suppression equipment in the event of an emergency. Plantings should be limited to carefully spaced low-flammability species.

Zone 2. Low-flammability plant materials should be used here. Plants should be low-growing, and the irrigation system should extend into this section.

Zone 3. Place low-growing plants and well-spaced trees in this area, remembering to keep the volume of vegetation (fuel) low.

Zone 4. This furthest zone from the structure is a natural area. Selectively prune and thin all plants and remove highly flammable vegetation.

Source: www.firewise.org/pubs/checklists/fwlistsz.pdf.

Table 3-2.
Potential Mass and Energy Loading for the 13 Standard Fuel Models.

No.	Fuel Complex	Load kg/hectare	Energy Load GJ/hectare
	Grass & grass dominated		
1	Short grass	1660	32
2	Timber (grass & understory)	1100–4400	21–84
3	Tall grass	6700	124
	Chaparral & Shrubs		
4	Chaparral	4400–11000	84–207
5	Brush	1100–2200	21–42
6	Dormant brush, wood slash	3500–5700	62–104
7	Southern rough	2400–4200	47–79
	Timber litter		
8	Closed timber litter	2400–5700	42–104
9	Hardwood litter	350–6400	6.2–120
10	Timber (litter & understory)	4400–11000	84–210
	Slash		
11	Light logging slash	3500–12400	62–230
12	Medium logging slash	8900–37000	168–690
13	Heavy logging slash	16000–62000	300–1100

Source: Pyne, Andrew, and Laven 1996.

with regard to wildfire safety standards: The fire then encounters more fuel than would naturally be available. In some cases, the homes contribute to the vertical spread of the fire from the ground to the surrounding canopy (Montague 2004a). Research by Cohen and Butler (1998) has repeatedly shown that structures often burn while surrounding vegetation survives.

This matters not only because the first two causes of ignition may still create some possibility for combustion, but also because defensible space cannot provide an effective buffer against firebrands. Fire-resistant construction can. The primary targets of opportunity are the roof, sides, eaves, soffits, and protruding features such as decks. Class A roofing assembly (which considers not only materials but how the roof is attached)

Homes present fires with densities of flammable materials much higher than the surrounding wildlands. A home catching fire can greatly intensify a wildfire in its immediate surroundings, including other nearby homes.

James Smalley

can protect the home from the likelihood of ignition from firebrands landing atop the home or being drawn inside the home through various openings. Nonflammable siding, including brick, stucco, and adobe construction, can also enhance fire safety, though to a lesser degree than fire-resistant roofing. Vinyl siding will resist combustion but may melt amid the heat of a wildfire. Fire-resistant eaves, fascias, and soffits, and/or the use of tightly knit wire mesh to enclose openings into the home, can all reduce the hazard exposure for the structure. Spark arrestors on chimneys are another effective form of structural mitigation. Each step serves to reduce the probabilities, but in combination they can all reduce hazard risks substantially.

Overall, it should be noted that there is no absolutely fire-proof solution, but the goal of Firewise construction is to reduce the probabilities so significantly as to ensure a high probability of survival. At a minimum, the mitigation measures can extend the ignition time sufficiently to allow the danger to pass rather than the home to be consumed in flames. Chapter 4 reviews how communities have designed and implemented specific strategies to achieve these goals.

CHAPTER 4

Wildfire Planning and Regulation:
Examples from the Field

This chapter examines on-the-ground examples of local plans and guidance documents for model plan elements, and a selection of local zoning and subdivision ordinances, including a number of national models.

COMPREHENSIVE PLAN ELEMENTS AND LOCAL SPECIFIC PLANS

This section describes a variety of model plan elements and a number of local wildfire plans. Most are directed at wildfire mitigation and are stand-alone documents; one is an element in a local comprehensive plan. In general, the plans reviewed here contain a number of common components, although they may differ in terminology:

- *A hazard assessment.* The communities mentioned here have used a process to identify areas prone to wildfires and, using a rating system, mapped and ranked them. For example, they have used aerial photos, historic records of wildfires, and contour maps in mapping general areas of risk. In establishing priorities, the analysis looks at types of fuel or vegetative types (these, of course, vary by region), topography, and weather.

- *A more specific risk assessment.* Individual areas at risk within the community undergo a risk assessment, using such factors as defensible space, roof types, proximity of buildings to each other, available water supply, adequacy of road systems for firefighting, and, in some cases, the ability of the existing fire department to respond to calls to evaluate levels of risk. This risk assessment, sometimes called a "vulnerability" assessment, produces a richer geographical picture of the potential for a wildfire to increase the loss of life, property, and natural resources. The evaluated areas are described in either narrative form or tabular form.

- *An institutional analysis.* In cases where a number of jurisdictions create a plan, such as for a county, the capacities and specializations of the various governmental organizations with an interest in wildfires are described.

- *A set of goals, policies, and implementing actions.* All the plans have specific goals and policies. Implementing actions take the form of adoption or modification of existing codes, public information initiatives, evacuation plans, enforcement initiatives, firefighter training and equipment purchases, land acquisition, and programs of vegetative removal or thinning.

What is lacking in many of the plans APA reviewed (including those not summarized below) is a connection to the local comprehensive plan.

What is lacking in many of the plans APA reviewed (including those not summarized below) is a connection to the local comprehensive plan. Development in the wildland-urban interface (WUI) is, of course, a direct consequence of land-use policy. Local land-use plans allow development at different levels of density in areas subject to wildfires, and land-use regulations implement those density ranges. The risk or vulnerability assessments will point to close proximity of buildings as a factor creating a high risk for damage. Yet many of the wildfire plans, which were developed by task forces, local fire departments, and advisory groups, and not by local planning commissions or planning departments, do not acknowledge the necessary link to a larger framework contained in the comprehensive plan, nor do they describe the inherent conflicts between the wildfire plan and comprehensive plan (although the reason for this may be institutional—fire departments may have more knowledge and experience with wildfires than with land-use planning).

The wildfire plans, in this sense, are remedial documents that attempt to mitigate the outcomes of land-use planning without trying to change its direction. For the purposes of dealing with wildfires, comprehensive plans need to distinguish between how they address undeveloped and developed lands because each calls for different strategies and priorities.

- In undeveloped areas, comprehensive plans most effectively address land-use density, circulation routing, and infrastructure requirements. For these areas, a comprehensive plan creates a schematic for the eventual settlement pattern, including level of density, points of access in subdivided areas, and water and fire station access. Each is important for wildfire planning purposes. The level of density affects the proximity of houses and structures to each other and therefore the potential for the spread of fires. Multiple points of access are important because they provide alternative routes to a wildfire-threatened or burning area if one route is blocked. They are created at the time land is subdivided, and the administration of subdivision controls ensures that street stubs to adjoining undeveloped properties eventually lead to full-fledged street connections when these adjacent lands are also subdivided. The presence of water lines from a central source will determine whether there will be hydrants with adequate water supply to fight fires. In addition, a comprehensive plan's community facilities element may designate general areas for the location of new fire stations so response times are adequate.

- For developed or subdivided lands (that is, lands with infrastructure installed, including streets, but with, perhaps, vacant lots or parcels), comprehensive plans should focus on policies for the management of hazards affecting individual public and private properties. These include policies for building materials, retrofitting existing structures, creating and maintaining defensible space, clearing dead and dying trees and related vegetation, and educating the public, among others. Specific examples of regulatory devices that implement these policies are discussed below.

The American Planning Association's Growing Smart ᔆᴹ Natural Hazards Element

The American Planning Association has published detailed model legislation for a natural hazards element of a comprehensive plan as part of its Growing Smart^SM Legislative Guidebook. The element, which appears in full with commentary as Appendix F of this report, is intended to establish a process to address all types of natural hazards, not solely wildfires. While the element is one a state legislature could adopt, with or without modifications, it can also serve as an outline for the development of administrative rules or guidelines for such an element.

The American Planning Association has published detailed model legislation for a natural hazards element of a comprehensive plan as part of its Growing Smart^SM Legislative Guidebook.

The Washington State Model for a Comprehensive Plan Element Addressing Natural Hazard Reduction

In Washington state, cities and counties in urban areas or areas rapidly urbanizing must prepare comprehensive plans under the state's Growth Management Act. The Washington Department of Community, Trade, and Economic Development publishes guidance for the various types of plan elements that constitute a local comprehensive plan. Washington communities have the option of preparing and adopting a plan element for natural hazard reduction, which covers flooding, landslides, and wildfires.

The Washington state manual contains a short section on planning and mitigation for wildfires. According to the manual, hazard reduction planning for fires requires:

- identification of the current hazard (characterization of fuel loads, topography, and meteorological patterns);

- modeling of potential future hazards based on forecasted or planned development or other types of land conversion, vegetation management plans and practices, and long-term meteorological forecasts (forecasting that now uses geographic information systems);

- identification of areas, structures, and people at risk from these hazards, and the likelihood and severity of such risk; and

- identification of resources available for fire response and recovery and documentation of shortfalls in these responses. (Washington Department of Community, Trade, and Economic Development 1999, p. 3-41).

The Washington state manual also lists a variety of fire hazard mitigation strategies similar to the regulations described below: (1) fireproofing development, (2) controlling ignition—largely educational strategies about fire concerns and the necessity of activity restrictions, and (3) facilitating response for personnel and equipment (including access to suitable water supply).

The State of California Requirement for a Safety Element in Comprehensive Plans

California requires local governments to adopt multi-element comprehensive plans, known as "general plans." A safety element is one of the components. The California Governor's Office of Planning and Research publishes a monograph on fire hazard planning intended to guide cities and counties when incorporating fire hazard policies into the general plan. The monograph lays out in considerable detail the type of data to be collected and offers suggested language for potential policies to be included in the general plan. An appendix provides contact information and related Web sites and publications. For instance, the section on urban interface hazards stresses updating high fire hazard severity zone maps and undertaking a cost-benefit analysis of various hazard mitigation measures as opposed to fire suppression (California Governor's Office of Planning and Research 2003, p. 14-15). Glendale's safety element, described in the next section, offers a good example of how the guidelines are reflected in a local safety element.

The Glendale, California, General Plan Safety Element

Glendale's safety element in its general (i.e., comprehensive) plan contains a section on fire hazards. The element notes that, in the portions of the San Rafael Hills and the Verdugo and San Gabriel Mountains within the city limits, the presence of flammable vegetation, steep topography, and limited access results in a high-hazard area constituting nearly two-thirds of the city land area, most of it in the north and northwest parts of Glendale (City of Glendale 2003, p. 3-9).

Because the portion of the city subject to wildfire hazards is so large, the element does not incorporate area-specific risk assessments. Indeed, Glendale's current programs of hazard mitigation are citywide, rather than specific to designated areas. For example, the city, according to the element, has adopted ordinances requiring all new roofs and re-roofs amounting to more than 25 percent of the original roof be constructed of Class A roofing materials. In addition, internal fire sprinklers are mandatory in all new residential one- and two-family structures. Under a fuel modification ordinance, Glendale requires property owners to maintain a defensible space around properties; the fire department conducts annual inspections of residences and lots to ensure compliance.

CITY OF GLENDALE, CALIFORNIA: GOAL 4 RELATED TO FIRE HAZARDS

Goal 4—Reduce the loss of life, injury, private property damage, infrastructure damage, economic loses, social dislocation, and other impacts resulted from fire hazards.

Policy 4-2: The City shall require that all new development in areas with high fire hazard incorporate fire-resistant landscaping and other fire hazard reduction techniques into the project design in order to reduce the fire hazard.

Program 4-2.1: The City shall encourage residents to plant and maintain drought-resistant, fire-resistant landscape species to reduce the risk of brush fire and soil erosion in areas adjacent to canyons, and develop stringent site design and maintenance standards for areas with high fire hazard or soil erosion potential.

Program 4-2.2: Fuel management plans shall be required for all new development in areas subject to wildfires.

Program 4-2.5: The City shall consider fire safety issues during revisions to the Zoning Ordinance.

Program 4-2.8: The City shall enforce a Class A roofing ordinance or better for residential and commercial developments. Residents with existing wood-shingle or unrated roofing materials shall be encouraged to upgrade to fire-resistive building materials, including fire-resistive eaves and awning.

Source: Glendale 2003, 3–11 to 3–12.

The plan contains a list of goals, policies, and programs on fire hazards. Goal 4 and the policy and programs related to it are provided in the sidebar.

The Okeechobee County, Florida, Wildland Fire Mitigation Plan

Of the various local plans we reviewed, the Okeechobee County Wildland Fire Mitigation Plan offers a unique strategic and institutional approach. Overseeing the plan was a technical advisory committee from city, county, emergency management, nonprofit, and property owner groups, assisted by a consultant. The plan's chief components are:

1. *A wildland fire risk analysis.* The county considered 11 different fire risk assessment systems as a basis for the plan. It finally adopted the Florida Department of Forestry's system, which in turn is based on the National Fire Protection Association 1144 publication, "Protection of Life and Property from Wildfire" (see discussion below). This system was used to evaluate and rank through field surveys 27 subdivisions that were identified through aerial photography as being in or adjacent to WUI areas (see Figure 4-1). Data from the evaluation were entered into a geographic information system.

   Three types of evaluations resulted. The first grouped the subdivisions into five risk classes (i.e., low hazard, moderate hazard, high hazard, very high hazard, and extreme hazard) (see Figure 4-2).

   The second evaluation gauged fire risk solely on adequacy of defensible space around buildings; the less defensible space, the greater the risk (see Figure 4-3).

   The third evaluation assessed risk resulting from the nature of the vegetative fuels in the area (see Figure 4-4).

Figure 4-1. Okeechobee County Field Survey of 27 Subdivisions.

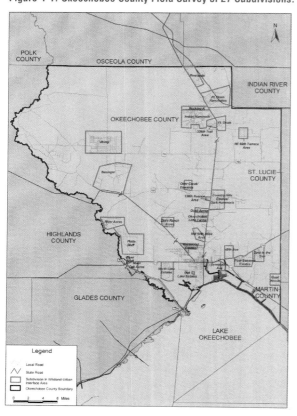

Figure 4-2. Ranking of Subdivisions into Hazard Classes.

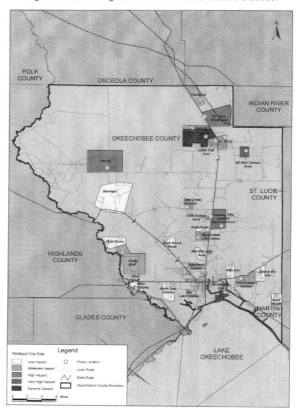

Figure 4-3. Gauging Fire Risk on the Basis of Defensible Space.

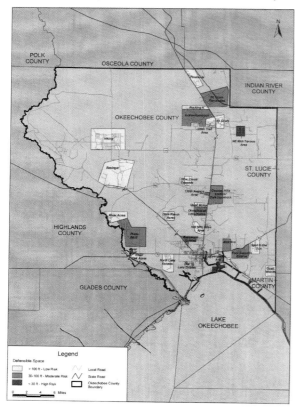

Figure 4-4. Gauging Risk on the Basis of Vegetative Fuels.

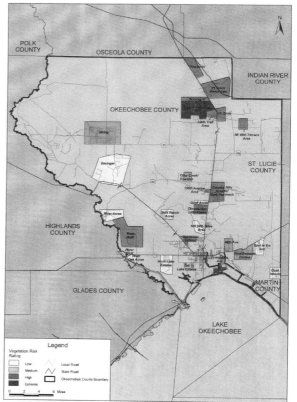

Source: Continental Shelf Associates Inc.

2. *A vulnerability survey.* This yielded a written description of each subdivision and, in some cases, photographs. A sample from one evaluation minced no words: "The absence of a readily available water supply, large adjacent areas of wildlands, neglected undeveloped lots, and medium- to high-risk vegetation contributed to the overall wildland fire risk in this area" (Okeechobee County 2003, p. 25). The photograph below shows the nature of the high-hazard vegetation in the area.

3. *Relationship to local comprehensive plan and environmentally significant areas.* The Okeechobee plan does relate wildfire risk to the future growth area designation contained in the county plan. It also identifies the relationship of WUI subdivision to endangered species and/or state-designated land areas containing unique natural resources, known as "Florida Forever Lands" and Florida Managed Areas (areas managed for biodiversity protection or multiple uses, including recreational use). Despite the recognition of this relationship, the Okeechobee plan does not recommend any changes to future land-use or growth area designations, but does acknowledge a need for the county comprehensive plan and development regulations to be amended.

   In a section of the plan assessing the role of the Okeechobee Department of Planning and Development, it comments that the county comprehensive plan "does not contain any policies that specifically address wildland fire" (p. 104). It then points to various sections of the county comprehensive plan—land use, infrastructure, conservation, intergovernmental coordination, and capital improvements—that should consider the wildland fire threat. Similarly, the plan observes that the county's development regulations do not contain specific language on wildfire and points to several possible sections (viz., those dealing with overlay and floating zones, cluster, transferable development rights, natural resource protection standards, and construction and design standards) that could be revised (p. 104).

4. *Institutional analysis.* The plan contains a very thorough review of agencies and organizations with an interest in wildland fire mitigation. Here the

Typical high-hazard vegetation in the Country Club Hills Estates/Dark Hammock Subdivision, Okeechobee County, Florida.

Continental Shelf Associates Inc.

analysis extends to the Florida Department of Forestry; state parks; the county itself, including administrative divisions; the water and wastewater utility authority; electrical companies; the water management district; the county chamber of commerce; and homeowner associations.

5. *Mitigation options.* The plan sets forth a series of carefully stated mitigation options and, in each case, assesses their applicability to the county, the cost, feasibility, public acceptance, and environmental consequences. The mitigation options are presented for parcels and single structures, neighborhoods and subdivisions, and institutions. Options include:

- Ignition reduction: public education and arson programs aimed at reducing the number of intentionally or accidentally (human) caused wildfires.

- Fuel reduction: prescribed burnings, mechanical fuels reduction, and herbicidal treatments to reduce available fuel.

- Exposure mitigation: fire-safe building standards, land-use planning and zoning measures, and insurance policy conditions intended to reduce exposure.

- Fire suppression: increasing the response capabilities of the fire service by government, community, or the individual property owner.

Other options include better forest management, enhanced technology (such as global positioning systems) and cooperative agreements among jurisdictions, such as fire departments.

The Santa Barbara, California, Wildland Fire Plan

Santa Barbara's Proposed Wildland Fire Plan (City of Santa Barbara 2003) is one of the most systematic and clearly written of the local plans reviewed in the course of the study. The area, notes the plan, experiences a major wildland fire on the average of every 10 years. Among them were:

These homes were among more than 600 structures destroyed in the 5,000-acre "Paint Fire" in 1990 in Santa Barbara. The housing development is at the intersection of Camino del Rio and Camino del Retiro. Most homes in the area were destroyed by the wind-driven fire.

Keith Cullom

- the 1964 Coyote Fire that burned 67,000 acres, destroyed 106 homes, and resulted in one death;

- the 1971 Romero Canyon fire that burned 14,500 acres, destroyed four homes, and resulted in four deaths;

- the 1977 Sycamore Canyon Fire that burned 805 acres and destroyed 195 homes with a property loss of $26.0 million; and

- the 1990 Painted Cave fire that burned 4,900 acres; destroyed 479 homes, with a property loss of $290.0 million; and resulted in one death.

The 1977 fire marked a shift from primarily suppression and prevention of wildfires to a greater emphasis on mitigation of the hazards and risks that make the area, which is characterized by steep, rocky terrain and covered with highly flammable chaparral vegetation, subject to fire.

Several aspects of this highly detailed plan deserve comment. The first is the hazard assessment. ArcView, Spatial Analyst, and Model Builder software from Environmental Systems Research Institute (ESRI) were used to complete a composite hazard assessment map for the study area. Using Spatial Analyst, three data layers were combined to classify hazard areas: slope, aspect, and fuel. The analysis assigned a value to each cell within a data layer. Values ranged from 1 to 10. For slope, the greater the percentage, the higher the value. For aspect or orientation, the values were highest for lands facing the southeast, south, and southwest. For fuel, low-moisture vegetation, such as heavy chaparral, dormant brush, and mixed conifers, received the highest scores. The relative values are shown in Table 4-1.

Model Builder software was applied to combine the three hazard data layers to produce a map that showed the results of the hazard assessment.

The second notable aspect is the risk analysis itself, which discloses the vulnerabilities of the four fire-hazard zones. For example, one of the highest risk areas, the "Extreme Foothill Zone" located along the northern boundary of Santa Barbara, was the site of the 1965 and 1977 fires. The

Table 4-1.
Composite Hazard Assessment Ratings for Santa Barbara

Slope	Value	Aspect	Value	Fuel	Value
0–10%	1	Flat	1	Light grass	1
11–20%	4	North	1	Trees and grass	1
21–30%	7	Northeast	1	Heavy chaparral	10
31–40%	9	East	7	Light brush	5
> 40%	10	Southeast	7	Dormant brush	10
		South	10	Hardwood overstory	7
		Southwest	10	Mixed conifer	10
		West	5	Mixed conifer— heavy	10
		Northwest	5	Urban fuel	1
				Agricultural lands	1
				Water	0
				Barren/rock/other	0

Source: City of Santa Barbara, Calif.

Santa Barbara County firefighters battle the 7,500-acre Gaviota fire in June 2004. They improve defensible space by using a chain saw to separate fuel from property and cutting tree limbs threatening a structure. Flames destroyed one building in this school complex while firefighters successfully prevented involvement in several other structures.

Keith Cullom

combination of heavy fuels, long response times (the area is outside the Santa Barbara Fire Department's four-minute response time), limited water supply, smaller residential roads that do not meet access standards, and historic fire weather patterns are all factors that relate to high risk. On the other hand, in contrast to other hazard areas, only one of the 138 structures identified had a combustible roof (e.g., wood shakes or similar combustible material).

The plan also includes a detailed vegetation management plan for city-owned property. The plan emphasizes hand cutting and chipping, so as to result in minimal ground disturbance, and prescribed burning where dry grass is left standing and then ignited over a small area not greater than an acre. It stresses that this type of work must be done on a scheduled basis.

Finally, the plan includes a draft interagency evacuation plan, which deals with operations issues. It separates the high-hazard areas into 26 evacuation areas determined by major canyons and road systems, and shows evacuation routes and fire response routes that may be used by fire personnel.

An omission in this plan is its lack of relationship to the city's comprehensive plan. As noted above, this is a common problem in many of the plans reviewed as part of the study.

The Ashland, Oregon, Community Wildfire Protection Plan (CWPP)

The Ashland Community Wildfire Protection Plan (CWPP) (City of Ashland 2004) is one of the first local plans developed and adopted in response to the federal Healthy Forests Restoration Act of 2003 (HFRA) (see the discussion of this law in Chapter 1). Under the HFRA, a CWPP "identifies and prioritizes areas for hazardous fuel reduction treatments and recommends the types and methods of treatment on federal and nonfederal land that will protect one or more at-risk communities and essential infrastructure; and recommends measures to reduce structural ignitability throughout the at-risk community."

An "at-risk community" is one within the vicinity of federal lands at high risk from wildfire, as defined by federal rules, or a group of homes and other structures with basic infrastructure and services (such as utilities and collectively maintained transportation routes) within or adjacent to federal land in which conditions are conducive to a large-scale wildland fire disturbance event that would pose a significant threat to human life or property. A CWPP must be "agreed to by the applicable local government, local fire department, and state agency responsible for forest management, in consultation with interested parties and the federal land management agencies managing land in the vicinity of the at-risk community" (HFRA, Section 101). Thus, the CWPP's intent is to get the key federal agencies, such as the U.S. Forest Service and the Bureau of Land Management, involved in a collaborative effort to address wildfire hazards surrounding communities adjoining federal lands like national forests and parks. Communities with CWPPs receive priority for federal funding for "authorized hazardous fuel reduction projects" (HFRA, Section 103).

In Ashland, the city forestlands commission compiled the CWPP, working in conjunction with local conservation groups, individual citizens, and city staff members. The CWPP pulls together in one document various elements of Ashland's wildfire protection strategy. Like the other plans reviewed as part of this study, the Ashland plan contains an inventory and assessment of lands in the WUI, a fuels-reduction program administered by the fire department, a discussion of codes and ordinances, and an assessment of infrastructure capacity, fire response, and post-fire recovery. The plan also contains materials on wildfire protection for homeowners.

One of the innovative features of the plan is a proposal to the U.S. Forest Service for a "forest resiliency alternative" for the Upper Bear Creek area. The alternative was proposed by an ad hoc group of volunteers that assisted the city in the plan. In essence, this highly detailed alternative calls for a different long-term strategy for forest management in the watershed area to reduce the likelihood of wildfire by changing the mix of vegetation. Under the proposal, the Forest Service would reduce primarily small-diameter fuels and density of understory seedlings, saplings, and poles to reduce ladder fuels, thin from below to create more open conditions, using prescribed fire where appropriate to reduce existing fuels, and planting or maintaining particular species in certain parts of the basin to maintain and restore forest diversity (for example, by planting hardwoods in lieu of conifers because they sprout and hold soil after a fire and by thinning out faster-growing conifers around hardwoods to provide more sunlight).

The Ashland plan contains a schedule of action items including:

- sponsoring a wildfire home safety tour emphasizing homes with good defensible space, fire-resistant landscaping, and fire-safe construction;

- developing and enforcing a fire-safe landscaping ordinance for new and existing structures;

- maintaining a staff position to manage WUI fuels reduction, to liaison with federal agencies, and to promote wildfire home safety;

- conducting wildfire evacuation drills in different neighborhoods each year;

- maintaining grant-funded thinning projects over time; and

- evaluating water-flow capabilities in WUI neighborhoods under simulated worst-case fire conditions, identifying those with potential problems, and suggesting mitigation measures.

Finally, the plan commits the city's forestlands commission to a twice-yearly review of progress on the plan's proposals. One limitation of this plan is its lack of connection to the city's overall comprehensive plan, a document required by Oregon law. Again, this is a common omission of the local wildfire plans APA reviewed.

ZONING ORDINANCE AND SUBDIVISION PROVISIONS, INCLUDING MODELS

This section digests a variety of model codes and standards, as well as local ordinances affecting building permits, site plans, subdivisions, and lot splits or partitions. In each analysis, we describe, where appropriate, the entire regulatory structure or unique features meriting the reader's attention. Ordinance provisions described relate to:

- designation of WUI, including criteria;
- administration of permitting;
- enforcement;
- appeals;
- requirements for application;
- vegetative management plans;
- fire control plans;
- public disclosure and information requirements;
- incentives; and
- standards, including those for access, fuel reduction, water supply, and construction.

The National Fire Protection Association's Standard for the Protection of Life and Property from Wildfire

The National Fire Protection Association (NFPA) has issued "Protection of Life and Property from Wildfire," which establishes standards used to provide minimum planning, construction, maintenance, education, and management elements for the protection of life, property, and other values threatened by wildland fire. Its provisions are similar to the International Code Council (ICC) model code described below. In particular, it contains measurable standards for access, ingress, egress, evacuation, and building design, location, and construction. It also includes a series of appendices used to assess wildland fire risk for a particular home or subdivision.

This standard may be adopted with or without amendments by municipalities, counties, or states. States adopting it include Florida (NFPA 299, 1997 Edition), California (by reference as part of NFPA 5000, a comprehensive building code), and Washington, with states as diverse as Pennsylvania, Montana, North Carolina, Colorado, Minnesota, and New Mexico using the hazard assessment checklist as the basis for their activities. Hundreds of local governments have also adopted it by reference or with adaptations, or use the hazard assessment checklist. These include Clark County, Washington; Douglas County, Colorado; and the Central Yavapai Fire District in Arizona. (See the searchable National Wildfire Programs Database at http://www.wildfireprograms.usda.gov/ for all participants.)

Particularly notable about this model is its description of a multiagency operational plan for the protection of lives and property during a wildfire, which goes beyond the typical land-use and building requirements most wildfire ordinances contain. Responsibility for preparing the plan may apparently differ from community to community. The operational plan must contain command, training, community notification and involvement, evacuation, and mutual assistance elements. These elements ensure a coordinated response among the various agencies and organizations, including fire departments, social service agencies, the local media, and law enforcement.

The International Code Council *International Urban-Wildland Interface Code*
ICC has published a comprehensive *International Urban-Wildland Interface Code* (ICC 2003), intended to bridge the gap between enforcement of the International Building Code and International Fire Code, also released by ICC, by mitigating the hazards of wildfires. The code contains seven chapters and eight appendices. Chapters cover administration, definitions, WUI areas and requirements, special building construction regulations, fire-protection requirements, and referenced standards. Communities around the country adopt the code, often with minor modifications to reflect local conditions.

Under the code, the local legislative body designates the WUI area within its jurisdiction based on findings of fact concerning climate, topography, vegetative character, and other characteristics affecting the area. The code requires the area to be recorded on maps and filed with the local government clerk. The code official must reevaluate and recommend modification to the interface area at least once every three years or more often if necessary.

A permit is required for buildings or structures in the WUI area, unless the activity is covered by permits issued under the building or fire code. A variety of plans accompany the permit application: a site plan showing, among other things, topography, vegetation, types of ignition-resistant building construction, and roof classifications; a vegetation management plan; and a fire protection plan, where required by the code official.

The code establishes minimum standards for buildings and structures in the interface area for emergency vehicle access and water supply, summarized below:

- *Emergency access* (see Chapter 4 of the code). The intent of the access requirements is to ensure that vehicle operators can find the building or structure in the case of fire or emergency, and emergency vehicles can maneuver around the area where a fire is located and get close to the buildings or structures. Driveways, 12 feet wide with an unobstructed height of 13.5 feet, must be provided when the exterior wall of a building is 150 feet from a fire apparatus access road. Turnarounds on driveways must be installed when the driveway is longer than 200 feet and less than 20 feet in width. The turnaround must be not less than 30 feet for the inside radius and not less than 45 feet for the outside radius. The fire apparatus access road itself must be an all-weather road with a minimum of 20-foot width and a clear height of 13.5 inches. The standards provide that the access road be designed to accommodate the loads and the turning radii of fire apparatus. Dead-end roads must incorporate a turnaround that the code official approves. The grade on driveways and roads is not to exceed 12 percent or the maximum approved by the code official. All roads must be marked with road identification signs, as must all fire protection equipment and hydrants. All buildings must have permanently posted address signs, placed at each driveway entrance, visible from both directions of travel along the road.

- *Water supply* (see Chapter 4 of the code). The code calls for approved water supplies for the use of fire protection and suppression. The water source must be located not more than 1,000 feet from the building or structure. For one- and two-family dwellings with a fire area not exceeding 3,600 square feet, the water supply must be 1,000 gallons/minute for a duration of 30 minutes. For larger dwellings, the water supply must be 1,500 gallons/minute for the same minimum duration. Buildings other than one- and two-family dwellings must have a water supply of not less than 1,500 gallons per minute for a duration of two hours.

Table 4-2.
Required Defensible Space

Urban-Wildland Interface Area	Fuel Modification Distance (in feet)
Moderate hazard	30
High hazard	50
Extreme hazard	100

Source: International Code Council 2003, Table 603.2.

The code uses a sliding distance scale, linked to the severity of the fire hazard, in setting standards for defensible space around new and existing structures. A "defensible space" is an "area either natural or manmade, where material capable of allowing a fire to spread unchecked has been treated, cleared, or modified to slow the rate and intensity of an advancing wildfire and to create an area for fire suppression operations to occur" (Chapter 2, Section 202). The code official is responsible for determining the nature of the severity. Appendix G of the code contains a fire-hazard rating form for this purpose. By evaluating subdivision design, vegetation, topography, roofing, fire protection water sources, existing building construction materials, and utilities, the code official can establish whether the hazard is moderate, high, or extreme. Table 4-2 shows the required defensible space standards of the code.

The State of Florida's Model Wildfire Mitigation Ordinance

The State of Florida has published an annotated model wildfire mitigation ordinance as part of a manual on best practices. Like the other ordinances reviewed in this chapter, this model focuses on risk reduction in defined wildfire hazard areas (Florida Department of Community Affairs 2004, 69–84). The ordinance assigns administrative and enforcement responsibilities to a wildfire mitigation official. A wildfire mitigation review board, which appoints the official, serves as an appellate body for landowners who wish to appeal the official's actions. The overlay district regulations are applicable to land-use changes, subdivisions, site plans, building permits, and all special use permits, including conditional uses and variances.

This model does not contain standards for identifying the WUI or high-risk areas within the interface. Rather, it states that the WUI delineation must be based on findings of fact and the high-risk areas must be based on data obtained from the Florida Wildfire Risk Assessment, the state-published *Wildfire Hazard Assessment Manual for Florida Homeowners*, or any study "supported by competent and substantial evidence."

While the standards for fuel reduction and defensible space maintenance are similar to other ordinances we reviewed, several interesting provisions in this model deserve consideration for application elsewhere:

- *Provisions for tree protection.* For communities with tree protection ordinances that would otherwise require local government permission to remove a tree, the ordinance waives those permit requirements where the tree is a highly flammable native or ornamental tree as listed in the ordinance, making it very desirable to remove it. Like other ordinances, it goes on to identify a series of recommended replacement trees that are less flammable (Florida Department of Community Affairs 2004, 79).

- *Public disclosure and education.* The model requires selling landowners, developers, and realtors to disclose in writing the fact an undeveloped property is within a high-risk area or an overlay district as well as the wildfire risks and potential nuisances posed by fuel management activities, including but not limited to the smoke produced by prescribed burning activities. Under these provisions, the wildfire mitigation official is to conduct public workshops, publish informational brochures, and make public announcements via the Internet and in written form on the risks posed by wildfires and the steps to be taken to mitigate potential damage.

- *Incentives.* The ordinance requires the local government to grant a one-time ad valorem tax exemption to all improvements to real property made by or for the purpose of wildfire mitigation and completed in accordance with the wildfire mitigation plan approved by the official. It should be noted that in some states it might be necessary to have clear authority from statutes for the local government to grant such exceptions. Another less dramatic incentive is a landowner awards program in which the local government recognizes landowners who have undertaken notable wildfire mitigation programs.

The Florida manual also contains a model vegetation management ordinance requiring any person owning, leasing, or controlling any land upon or adjacent to wildlands to reduce brush around such structures in order to establish an effective fuel break and to take other actions, such as keeping the roof and gutters free of flammable debris. If a violation is found, the violator has 60 days to correct the problem, or the local government may correct the violation and assess the property owner the cost as well as establish a lien on the property until that cost is paid. This provision is similar in purpose to the nuisance approach used in the North Port, Florida, ordinance described below.

Ashland, Oregon, Development Standards

Ashland, Oregon, has established a series of development standards for preliminary plats and applications to partition land containing designated wildfire areas. Such developments trigger the preparation of a "fire prevention and control plan" as part of the application process. These are reviewed by the fire chief as part of the record of the action. Such a plan must contain:

- an analysis of the wildfire hazards on the site as influenced by existing vegetation and topography;

- a map showing the areas to be cleared of dead, dying, or severely diseased vegetation;

- a map of the areas to be thinned to reduce the interlocking canopy of trees;

- a tree management plan showing the location of all trees to be preserved and removed on each lot (in the case of heavily forested parcels, only trees scheduled for removal must be shown);

- the areas of primary and secondary fuel breaks required to be installed around each structure as required by the code; and

- roads and driveways sufficient for emergency vehicle access and fire suppression activities, including the slope of all roads and driveways within the wildfire lands area (City of Ashland 2004, Section 18.62.090.A.3).

The hearing authority has the discretion to approve the plan and to impose conditions including:

- delineation of areas of heavy vegetation to be thinned and a formal plan for such thinning;

- clearing of sufficient vegetation to reduce fuel load;

- removal of all dead and dying trees; and

- relocation of structures and roads to reduce the risks of wildfire and improve the chances of successful fire suppression (Section 18.62.909.A.5).

The plan must be implemented prior to the issuance of building permits. For subdivisions, provisions for maintenance of the plan must be included in the covenants, with the City of Ashland named as a beneficiary of the covenants, restrictions, and conditions. For partitions, the property owner is responsible for maintaining the plan.

All new construction and any construction expanding the size of an existing structure must have a fuel break. A primary fuel break extends out a minimum of 30 feet from all structures or to the property line, whichever is less. Here the goal is to remove ground cover that will produce flame lengths in excess of one foot. The regulations require the fuel break's depth to be increased by 10 feet for each 10 percent increase in slope over 10 percent. Where surrounding landscape is owned and under the control of the property owner, a secondary fuel break extending 100 feet beyond the primary fuel break must be provided (Section 11.62.090.B).

The Hayward, California, WUI Guidelines

The Hayward, California, WUI guidelines contain a series of construction standards for certain areas of the Hayward Hills the city's fire department has designated as "urban/wildland interface zones." According to the guidelines, these areas typically include development sites adjoining steep slopes, open grass/brush lands, woodland and riparian zones, or major drainage swales. In such areas, existing vegetation may cause structures to be exposed to rapidly spreading fire that is difficult for the Hayward fire department to control (Hayward 1993, ii).

Hayward's guidelines differ according to structure categories. Category I structures are those structures located on sites where "maximum built-in fire protection measures are necessary due to nearby steep slopes or wildland fuel loading." These structures are to exceed minimum State of California Fire Safe Guidelines. Category II structures are those located in the balance of the WUI. These meet minimum California guidelines.

Hayward's fire department designates which sites or lots must comply with either the Category I or Category II standards. In some cases, developers may be required to obtain, at their expense, a qualified WUI fire management consultant to assist in this designation.

The guidelines address both construction standards and fuel management. Building construction standards, listed below, can be applied either to Category I ("I") or II structures ("II"), or both ("I & II").

1. Enclose all roof eaves (I).

2. Provide double-pane windows for exterior window (I).

3. Specify a one-hour fire-resistive rating or greater for exterior building material (I).

4. Within 10 feet of a structure, construct fences with an open wire mesh or noncombustible material to prevent fire from spreading to the structure (I).

5. Design roofs that comply with a "Class A" noncombustible roof rating as outlined in [California] State Building Code Section 3202, 1991 edition (do not use wood shake or treated wood shake roofs) (I & II).

6. Provide metal enclosures with one-quarter inch metal mesh screens on all attic vents (side vents) and basement vents (I & II).

7. Provide spark arrestors with one-quarter inch mesh screens on all chimneys (I & II). (Hayward 1993, 13).

The guidelines call for the establishment of a fuel management program and recommend, if feasible, the program be implemented by a homeowner association through covenants and restrictions applicable to the development. The program is to consist of:

1. *Homeowner education.* This includes preparation of a pamphlet on fire safety, the fire cycle, and the ecological factors related to fire.

2. *A shaded fuel break.* This interrupts the fire ladder or the transfer of fire from the ground (via shrubs and ground covers) to tree canopies. In such an area, brush and selected understory are removed from the ground, and lower limbs of trees are pruned back.

3. *"Mosaic islands" of brush and shrubs.* In such areas, stands are selectively thinned—from 60 to 70 percent removed—to reduce fuel loading and break up the continuity of the fuel bed.

4. *Fire-resistant plants for domestic and replacement planting.* The guidelines recommend a series of species.

5. *Establishment of fuel management zones.* The guidelines propose four levels of zones to limit the exposure of a structure to radiant heat and debris from an advancing fire. Zone 1 is the minimum 30-foot firebreak

Figure 4-5. Fuel Break, Before and After

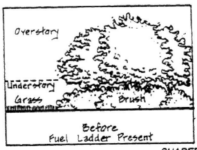 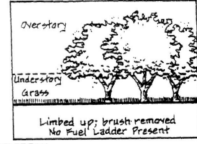

SHADED FUELBREAK

Source: City of Hayward, Calif.

Figure 4-6. Mosaic Islands

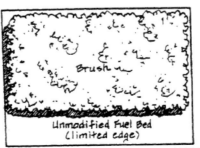 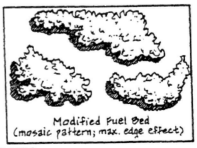

MOSAIC ISLANDS

Source: City of Hayward, Calif.

Figure 4-7. Fuel Management Zones

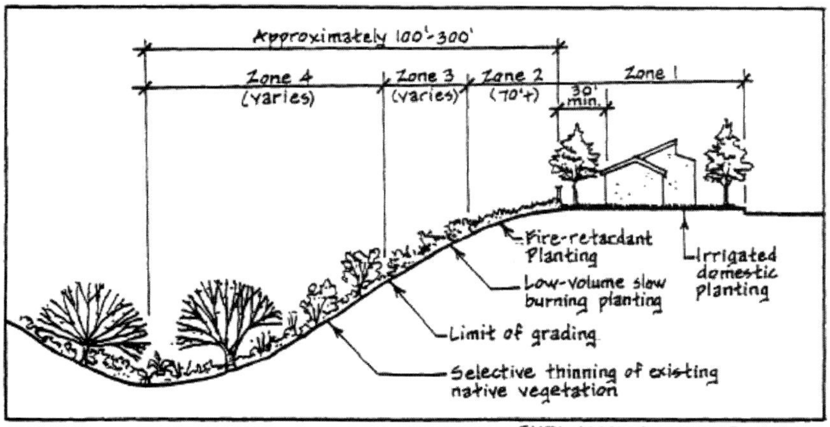

Source: City of Hayward, Calif.

immediately adjacent to the house or structure limited to fire-resistant species, trees with high canopies, and low-growing shrubs and ground covers. The guidelines call for the annual removal of dead leaves and the installation of an automatic irrigation system for domestic landscaping during hot, dry periods. Zone 2 is an additional firebreak of 70 feet or more that may be required depending on the fire department's judgment on the sufficiency of zone 1. Zone 3 is a fuel break transition zone. Here domestic plants should be low-growing, slow-burning, and low-volume species that blend with the landscape and require no water once established. Zone 4 is natural open space where fuels have been modified through shaded fuel breaks and mosaic islands to reduce fuel loading, fuel continuity, and fire ladders. Where a roadway abuts open space in such a zone, the guidelines recommend reducing or modifying vegetation for a minimum distance of 10 feet from the roadway.

The North Port, Florida, Environmental Code

North Port, Florida, has enacted Ordinance No. 86–206 as part of its environmental code. The ordinance is aimed at eliminating the accumulation of weeds and underbrush, unusable household items, junk vehicle parts, and other nuisance characteristics (including eliminating potential refuges for snakes, rats, and other vermin, and breeding places for mosquitoes). As part of its purpose statement, the ordinance particularly refers to the potential for creating a fire and/or health hazard. It applies to occupied and unoccupied lots; that is, lots with dwellings or structures on them, inhabited or uninhabited, as well as undeveloped lots. Thus, this law is not expressly a wildfire ordinance, but instead addresses wildfires through a nuisance rationale.

Section 4.01 of the ordinance provides:

> It shall be unlawful for any owner of an occupied or an unoccupied lot to permit the excessive growth of cultivated or uncultivated grass, weeds or underbrush in excess of 12 inches in height upon said lot. Shrubs, trees, bushes, or any other natural or cultivated species of foliage found and/or planted upon said lot and used for landscaping purposes shall be permitted to grow to its [sic] natural height, provided however, that such growth shall not become a fire or safety hazard to the neighboring premises nor shall such growth be permitted to grow beyond the legal confines of said lot so as to impinge upon the neighboring property and premises or upon a public right-of-way such as sidewalks and/or streets.

Similar provisions apply to undeveloped lots. The chief of the city's environmental division enforces the ordinance either by systematic inspection or upon receiving a written complaint, which then triggers an inspection. Once an ordinance violation is verified, the chief issues a violation notice, ordering compliance within a certain period. At the conclusion of the period, a second inspection is conducted. If the deficiency is not corrected, the chief refers the matter to a code enforcement compliance board for processing and adjudication.

The Clark County, Washington, Wildland Urban Interface/Intermix Ordinance

The Clark County, Washington, Wildland Urban Interface/Intermix Ordinance requires preventative measures in connection with subdivision, building permits, and other development applications in the interface/intermix area. It also establishes the criteria for mapping the areas subject to the regulation. Some parts of the county are simply included by reference to their legal description—the specific section and range number of a particular named township. Other areas are included because they satisfy slope, vegetative, and fire support criteria, as follows:

- Elevation in excess of 500 feet and one or more of the following conditions:
  - slope equal to or greater than 25 percent;
  - forest type vegetation; and
  - outside an organized fire protection district.

The ordinance language also clarifies the scope of application of the requirements: "Whenever the majority of a parcel lies within the established wildland-urban interface/intermix area, the entire parcel shall be included in the area."

The ordinance refers to National Fire Protection Association (NFPA) Standard 299, Protection of Life and Property from Wildfires, as amended, as one of the standards to be used in approving applications for permits (see discussion of the successor standard, NPFA 1144, above). Once an application is approved, the conditions must be recorded on the final plat

CHARACTERISTICS OF FIRE-RESISTIVE VEGETATION

Codes affecting development in the WUI may propose the planting of fire-resistive vegetation, which burns at a relatively low intensity and has slow rates of spread with short flame lengths. Characteristics of such vegetation include:

- Growth with little or no accumulation of dead vegetation, either on the ground or standing upright
- Nonresinous plants, such as willow, poplar, or tulip trees
- Low volume of total vegetation, such as a grass area as compared to a forest or shrub-covered land
- Plants that contain a large amount of water in comparison to their dry weight
- Drought-tolerant plants—deeply rooted plants with thick, heavy leaves
- Stands of plants without ladder fuels—fine, small branches and limbs between the ground and the canopy of overtopping shrubs and trees
- Plants requiring little maintenance
- Plants with woody stems and branches that require prolonged heating to ignite

Source: International Code Council 2003.

or binding site plan or attached to building permits or other approvals for development and construction.

Similar to the Florida model described above, an official, in this case the fire marshal, must make available pamphlets to builders and homeowners summarizing these code provisions as they regulate construction and explaining what actions are needed by homeowners to maintain their homes to comply with this code (Clark County 2004, Ch.15.13).

The Prescott, Arizona, Urban-Wildland Interface Code

Prescott, Arizona, has adopted the ICC Model Urban-Wildland Interface Code, described above. In doing so, it modified some of the code's language to fit the specifics of its area and to add detail to certain sections of the model. For example, the ICC code calls for the local government to incorporate findings of fact that serve as a justification for the designation of wildland areas. One of the aspects of the findings is to designate a specific fuel model—a description of the mix of potentially flammable vegetative materials. The nature of the fuel model affects the flame length and rate of spread, as described below:

> The seasonal climatic conditions during the late spring and early summer create numerous serious difficulties regarding the control of and protection against fires in the City of Prescott.
>
> Average maximum temperatures of 88.9 degrees in July
>
> Relative humidity: 10 to 15 percent in May and June
>
> 28 days of extreme fire weather conditions from end of April through July
>
> Live fuel moisture in chaparral from 61.8 percent in April to 86.4 percent in August. (Anything under 80 percent will burn)
>
> Fuel moisture in 1,000-hour fuels is 5 percent
>
> Winds: 35 to 40 miles per hour
>
> Numerous dry lightning strikes
>
> Prescott has predominantly fuel model 4 (chaparral), which is found in all of the "at risk neighborhoods." This includes oak brush (scrub oak) and manzanita.
>
> Utilizing fuel model 4 scenarios as an example, the rate of spread could be 721 feet per minute. The flame lengths could be 57 feet high. Burning brands can jump ahead of the fire for a distance of 2.1 miles and ignite additional fires. The fire could consume 5,641 acres in one hour and spread a distance of 8.1 miles. The perimeter of the fire would be 90,321 feet. This type of fire is uncontrollable by the on-duty fire forces due to lack of staffing and lengthy response times. This fire could result in a major structural conflagration. The fire could spread across the Prescott Basin at the interface (Prescott 2003, Section 6–2–2 (K)).

Further, the Prescott code amplifies the requirements for the vegetation management plan. The code requires that the modification of vegetative fuel—removal of slash, snags, other ground fuels, ladder fuels, and dead trees and the thinning of live trees—within 30 feet of the house or to the property line, whichever is less, be completed prior to any vertical construction. Beyond 30 feet and up to 150 feet of the house or property line, the vegetative fuel modifications must be completed before a certificate of occupancy can be issued (Section 6–2–2(FF)).

The code details requirements for the defensible space surrounding the structure. It prescribes the following defensible space practices:

- Decreasing the amount of flammable vegetation

- Increasing the amount of open space

- Increasing the moisture content of vegetation

Figure 4-8. Prescott Arizona Urban Wildlands Interface

Urban Wildlands Interface Map

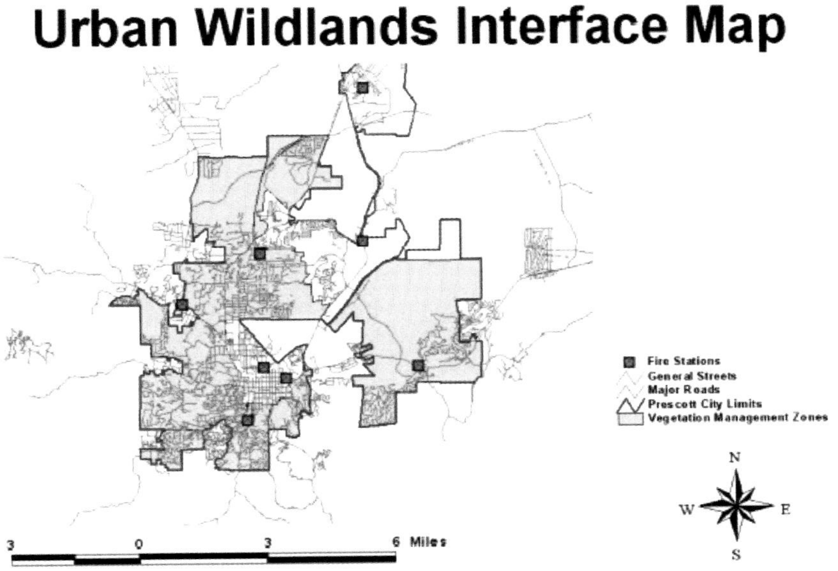

Source: Prescott 2003, Ordinance 4367, 12.

- Planting less flammable plants

- Rearranging existing plants

- Reducing trees to a maximum of 200 hydrated or 85 nonhydrated, healthy trees per acre with understory pruned and maintained

- Removing all combustible materials and vegetation from under decks

- Continuing maintenance of the area

- Maintaining the defensible space requirements by the homeowners association and/or owner of the property (Section 6–2–2(FF)).

The Jefferson County, Colorado, Wildfire Hazard Overlay District

Provisions relating to wildfires in Jefferson County, Colorado, appear in its zoning code as a "W-H Wildfire Hazard Overlay District." The overlay district does not affect the uses permitted in the underlying zoning district. However, an applicant for a building permit must either create defensible space and associated fuel break thinning around the dwelling, or submit a wildfire mitigation site plan for review and approval as a special exception (conditional use) by the board of adjustment. The ordinance adopts design standards and criteria contained in a fact sheet from Colorado State University's Cooperative Extension. Sites must also satisfy access standards contained in the zoning code and must be inspected by the Colorado State Forest Service or other qualified inspector before a building permit may be issued. In addition, a final inspection of the site must be conducted prior to the issuance of a certificate of occupancy, a document verifying that activities carried out under the building permit have been completed as approved. Persons disputing whether a certificate of completion can be issued, the location of a wildfire zoning district boundary, or the nature of conditions imposed on a site by the county are given a "reasonable opportunity to present their case to the Zoning Administrator or his/her appointed designee and shall submit forestry and topographic evidence to support such contests" (Jefferson County 2002, Section 49).

The Pinetop-Lakeside, Arizona, Forest Health and Fire Protection Code

The City of Pinetop-Lakeside code relating to forest health and fire protection contains detailed guidance on the establishment of a three-zone plan to satisfy the defensible space requirements on all parcels whether there is a building or structure and for vacant parcels of less than two acres. The code describes a set of mandatory and recommended actions for property in each zone. Most notable is the reduction of tree density through on-site thinning to lower risk from fires.

A. **Zone 1:** Zero feet to 10 feet from buildings, structures, decks, etc.

1. Required Zone 1 Fuel Modification:
   a. Remove fuel ladders and reduce non-fire-resistant brush, leaving primarily fire-resistant specimens.
   b. Remove and destroy all insect infested, diseased, and dead trees to prevent spread to healthy vegetation.
   c. Remove all dead plant material from the ground that may create fuel ladders or contribute to the spread of fire.
   d. Where applicable, trim coniferous trees to where the lowest branches or canopy are above the roofline and a minimum of ten feet from chimneys or other sources of ignition.
   e. Remove flammable debris from gutters and roof surfaces.
   f. Remove all combustible materials and vegetation from under decks. Non-fire-resistant vegetation within three feet of buildings, structures, and decks should be spaced to limit ignition from surrounding vegetation and the creation of fuel ladders.

2. Recommended Zone 1 Fuel Modification:
   a. Defensible space should be regularly maintained during periods of high fire danger.
   b. Provide adequate hydration for all vegetation.

B. **Zone 2:** Ten feet to 30 feet from buildings, structures, decks, etc.

1. Required Zone 2 Fuel Modification:
   a. Remove all ladder fuels and dead material.
   b. Remove and destroy all insect infested, diseased, and dead trees to prevent spread to healthy vegetation.

2. Recommended Zone 2 Fuel Modification:
   a. Zone 2 defensible space shall be maintained at least annually.
   b. Create separation between trees, tree crowns and other plants based on fuel type, density, slope, and other topographical conditions that may adversely affect fire behavior.
   c. Reduce continuity of fuels by creating clear space around brush or planting groups.
   d. Control erosion and sedimentation from exposed soils through terracing, gravel beds, rocks, or other appropriate ground cover. Emphasis is placed on slopes greater than 20 percent gradient, in which case, additional vegetation treatment may be required.
   e. Remove all but one inch of pine needle or leaf droppings. It is important to leave a layer of decomposing plant material to maintain adequate moisture levels for further decomposition and plant hydration.

C. **Zone 3:** Thirty feet to 100 feet from buildings, structures, decks, etc. where slopes do not exist and undeveloped lots are less than two acres.

1. Required Zone 3 Fuel Modification:
   a. Remove all ladder fuels and dead material.

b. Thin coniferous trees to achieve an overall average density of not more than one hundred trees or sixty square feet basal area per acre. ["Basal area" is a measurement of tree density. The basal area is the cross-sectional area of a tree 4.5 feet above ground. The basal area of all trees in a given land area describes the degree to which an area is occupied by trees and is generally expressed in square feet per acre. The basal area calculation is: X^2 multiplied by .005454, where X equals tree diameter in inches at 4.5 feet above ground, or diameter at breast height (dbh). For example, the basal area of a 12-inch dbh tree is calculated as follows: $12^2 \times .005454 = .7854$ square feet (City of Pinetop-Lakeside Code, Section 16.117.030.1, 2004).]

c. Remove and destroy all insect infested, diseased, and dead trees to prevent spread to healthy vegetation.

2. Recommended Zone 3 Fuel Modification:
   a. Zone 3 defensible space should be maintained at least annually. (Pinetop-Lakeside 2004, Section 16.117.070)

The Yakima County, Washington, Urban-Wildland Interface Code

Yakima County, Washington, has adopted, in modified form, the ICC Urban-Wildland Interface Code, described above. Among the modifications is a simplified way of classifying the lands within WUI areas. The county's ordinance does this on the basis of slope, distance to a county road, and whether the property is within a fire district, but stresses that risk-factor classifications are not absolute. Those classifications are as follows:

- *Non-Rated.* Slope less than 8 percent, within one mile of a county road, and inside a fire district

- *Moderate Hazard.* Slope greater than 8 percent, within one mile of a county road, and inside a fire district

- *High Hazard.* Slope greater than 8 percent, more than one mile from a county road, and inside a fire district

- *Extreme Hazard.* Slope greater than 8 percent, more than one mile from a county road, and outside a fire district. (Yakima County 2001, Section 9)

CHAPTER 5

Big Issues in Planning for Wildfires

Wildfires have become the focus of growing concern among a number of professional disciplines that in various ways share responsibility for protecting the public safety. These include firefighters, foresters, elected officials, architects, engineers, and—most important for the purposes of this report—planners. As fire and the built environment come together in new forms of development labeled the wildland-urban interface (WUI), the potential for harm to life, resources, and quality of life has grown. This report has addressed the ways in which planning can be used to promote effective and realistic solutions to that potential harm.

In this final chapter, the report brings together the big-picture issues and long-term strategies that need to be addressed to craft responses to problems likely to grow in the foreseeable future. The focus in this chapter is on wildfire issues as addressed by state and local government, a partnership of all levels of government along with public and private organizations, and, to a limited extent, through voluntary action.

Building on the discussion in Chapter 1 on why people build and live in the WUI, this chapter begins with a continued discussion of the perceptions and attitudes that prompt the decision to build and of how people's perceptions of wildfire hazards can be altered to produce behavioral change. The chapter next turns to an analysis of institutional and legal/political factors impeding effective planning responses to wildfires. The chapter concludes by proposing a series of strategies in three areas synthesizing the information about practices. The strategies include:

- Conducting wildfire planning in a comprehensive planning context

- Conducting a program of regulation and enforcement that stresses continuous individual responsibility by homeowners and property owners

- Conducting an effective ongoing program of education and outreach to affected residents and property owners

Each discussion of a recommended strategy is accompanied by a discussion of tools and techniques, and their advantages and limitations.

INFLUENCING PERCEPTIONS AND ATTITUDES

As Chapter 1 noted, many people are aware of the risks associated with their choice to live in the WUI. They balance perceived risks and benefits and find greater weight on the positive side. Those calculations probably rarely meet the rigorous tests of professional risk managers. Nonetheless, social science research indicates there is considerable, though not enormous, latitude for influencing those perceptions, and with them, behaviors and choices that affect the level of risk associated with living in wildfire-prone areas.

Perception of the benefits and risks entailed in these choices certainly is rooted in these personal preferences. The question is To what extent are

This scene from northern California shows thinned vegetation around the structures on both upward and down slopes. Note the dense vegetation elsewhere. The problem with this area is that water would have to be brought in by tenders, and the road network would be a hindrance to fire apparatus in times of fast-moving fire. The area is outside a subdivision whose covenants prohibited the removal of trees and vegetation, living or dead, particularly trees six inches or more in diameter regardless of location.

James Smalley

these perceptions malleable? To what extent can they be influenced through public education and outreach, or through experience, and which influences are most effective?

Past experience with natural hazards is one factor that has been studied in a number of circumstances, of which wildfire is but one. Surveys of homeowners in Minnesota and Florida, for example, found that most homeowners used past or recent experience to explain their personal assessment of the risks involved. Another significant factor was the experience of others familiar to them (Nelson et al. 2002). The power of anecdotal evidence has its limits, however, in persuading homeowners of the reality of a risk yet to materialize within their experience of an area. Still, the same study found large majorities in both states who believed their homes were at risk from wildfires.

Nelson et al. (2002), Vogt (2002), and Vogt, Winter, and Fried (2002) all found regional variations in attitude toward specific types of wildland fire mitigation related to homeowners' experiences with those methods. In Florida, for instance, homeowners exhibited substantial tolerance for and support of prescribed burns as a mitigation tool largely because they had witnessed its extensive and responsible use by agencies such as the Florida Division of Forestry, and thus had learned to trust that officials knew what they were doing to effective address the problem. In other states with less experience with prescribed burns but greater exposure to other tools for managing vegetation levels (for example, mechanized brush removal), support levels were higher for those techniques with which residents were familiar and for which they had learned to trust the agencies performing the mitigation tasks. In other words, public trust can be built through successful programmatic experience. That said, experience in many western states might suggest there is a greater psychological distance from, and hence less trust of, federal agencies as compared to state and local forest and fire agencies. To the extent this is true, Florida may benefit from the simple fact that the state has relatively few federal lands, making state and local agencies the dominant players in wildfire planning and mitigation.

Two other factors differentiating homeowners' perceptions should be considered. One is the potential for differences between seasonal and permanent homeowners in wildland areas. While this subject is worth a great deal more study within particular jurisdictions, differences between these two groups have been widely noted in a number of areas. The potential for significant socioeconomic differences between permanent residents and vacationers and tourists is almost inherent in part because the ownership of a second home tends to require a certain level of affluence.

Exactly how that is reflected in attitudes toward risk, land-use planning, and government regulation generally remains to be seen. Vogt (2002), in a study of homeowners in wildland areas in parts of California, Colorado, and Florida, found that seasonal homeowners were generally more supportive of land-use planning than permanent residents, while the latter, concerned about the availability of year-round jobs, were typically more supportive of local economic development initiatives. For planners, however, this would seem to suggest a disconnect between those who actually vote locally and those most supportive of a stronger role for planning in addressing wildfire hazard mitigation. It is not an insurmountable challenge, and planning and economic development need not be conflicting goals, but it would seem prudent to be aware of such differences to the extent they exist.

The second factor undoubtedly triggered by increased reliance on telecommuting is the rising education level of WUI residents. While Pyne (1982) noted affluence as a factor in the new wave of settlers moving to

Experience in many western states might suggest there is a greater psychological distance from, and hence less trust of, federal agencies as compared to state and local forest and fire agencies.

Table 5-1.
Demographic Characteristics of Permanent and Seasonal Residents in Wildfire Areas in California, Colorado, and Florida

	California (n = 295)		Colorado (n = 320)		Florida (n = 324)	
	Permanent (n = 119)	Seasonal (n = 176)	Permanent (n = 254)	Seasonal (n = 66)	Permanent (n = 267)	Seasonal (n = 57)
Gender						
Male	53	61	76	68	70	79
Female	47	39	42	32	30	21
Employment status						
Employed, full- or part-time	42	45	37	41	52	45
Self-employed	10	10	16	14	12	9
Retired	42	43	44	42	33	46
Other	6	32	3	3	3	0
Household income levels						
Less than $40,000	28	21	30	8	31	11
$40,000 to $79,999	43	33	47	34	48	39
$80,000 or more	29	46	23	58	21	50
Highest education level						
Jr. College or high school	16	21	23	11	44	30
College	61	52	44	47	43	32
Graduate school	23	27	33	42	13	38

Source: Vogt 2002.

interface areas in California, such as Malibu beginning in the 1950s, the more recent technological changes have introduced a wave of people to these areas who clearly have higher levels of education. Vogt's study of permanent and seasonal homeowners, part of which appears in Table 5-1, shows generally (though not consistently) higher income and education levels among seasonal residents in the three states, though relatively little difference in employment status.

Only Florida shows a significantly higher percentage of retirees. Perhaps because of their greater tenure in the affected areas, permanent homeowners scored much higher (except in Florida) in the frequency with which they had experienced or observed problems resulting from wildfires (Table 5-2).

FACTORS INFLUENCING BEHAVIOR

Why people choose to live in the WUI is one issue. How they behave with regard to managing their risks once they are there is another. The latter has been the object of a great deal of attention not only from researchers but also from local public officials and from others involved in various forms of public outreach and education, notably including the Firewise Communities training program. The idea that homeowner behavior can be altered to reduce risk significantly rests on the assumption that education and citizen involvement will make a difference. The effectiveness of wildfire mitigation within existing interface communities depends heavily on the validity of that assumption.

Fundamentally, there are three ways in which people's perceptions of wildfire hazards can be altered to produce behavioral change. One is a shift in their comparison of risks and benefits to more heavily emphasize the risk of wildfire, such that they conclude the risks outweigh the benefits that attract them to wildland areas. For existing residents of the interface, this would involve the wrenching conclusion they no longer wish to be

Table 5-2.
Frequency of Experience or Observation of Problems Resulting from Wildfires among Permanent and Seasonal Residents in California, Colorado, and Florida (in percent)

	California Permanent	Seasonal	Colorado Permanent	Seasonal	Florida Permanent	Seasonal
Observed effects of wildland fires on forests	85	68[a]	75	62[b]	70	72
Experienced smoke from a wildfire	82	45[a]	69	61	80	83
Personally witnessed a wildfire	80	56[a]	64	55	63	70
Experienced a road closure due to a wildland fire	77	44[a]	26	26	42	46
Felt fear or anxiety as a result of a wildland fire	57	35[a]	27	24	28	33
Friends, family, or neighbors suffered property damage from a wildland fire	29	10[a]	20	12	13	25[b]
Experienced discomfort or health problems from smoke caused by a wildland fire	19	9[b]	14	12	26	21
Suffered property damage from a wildland fire	5	1[a]	5	5	5	5
Been personally injured by a wildfire	3	1	2	0	1	7

Notes:
[a]Seasonal homeowners were significantly different from permanent homeowners at the p<.001 level.
[b]Seasonal homeowners were significantly different from permanent homeowners at the p<.05 level.
Source: Vogt 2002.

there, which would presumably cause them to relocate away from the area. Human nature, in the absence of a truly dispiriting disaster, would tend to work against such a conclusion. Moreover, people often lack viable options to rebuilding in the same location and thus return despite the proven dangers. This was the case in Oakland in the aftermath of the devastating 1991 fire (Schwab et al. 1998). Alternatively, such a conclusion could act to restrain potential newcomers, although it is harder to test such a hypothesis.

The second possible shift in behavior would affect the activity of those continuing to live in the WUI. Perceiving greater risk of wildfire, but short of relocating, they could conclude they need to undertake various mitigation measures to reduce their risk. This would require, first of all, some confidence in the efficacy of specific mitigation efforts, as a result of either persuasion or experience. For example, seeing a neighbor's home survive a fire because of metal roofing, fireproof soffits or siding, or the clearance of defensible space surrounding the home, while another home was consumed by fire after the owner failed to take such steps, might produce a perceptual shift resulting in greater cooperation with community-sponsored mitigation efforts and possibly in greater support for a revised building code to require the use of fire-retardant building materials.

Montague (2004a) states from experience with the Firewise Communities training program, "communities exposed to such programs as Firewise or FireSafe (a California initiative) are developing a foundational understanding of wildland fires that becomes entrenched when a significant wildland fire impacts their community, neighboring areas, or a similar type of community." What Montague goes on to suggest is this knowledge alters residents' perceptions of the event in ways that help them evaluate what works and what does not. This knowledge is similar in effect to the ways in which other scientific and technical knowledge alters our perception of astronomical events, seismic disturbances, or even the collapse of a building. Armed with such knowledge, people become more perceptive and analytical in ways they may not even fully realize. The University of Colorado's Natural Hazards Center has produced some valuable material regarding the effective communication of hazards with great potential utility to planners and others engaged in such efforts (see Mileti et al. 2004).

A third possibility, affecting those attuned to environmental health, is that some residents may perceive the consequences of previous development and forest management decisions in the ailing forest, for example in the visibility of drought stress among trees from competition for limited water. Responses to this perception could lead to wildfire mitigation activities arising primarily from a concern for restoring forest health. In ways similar to Montague's observation about foundational knowledge for risk assessment, a higher level of environmental knowledge could spur further action and better understanding with regard to forest health.

A crucial factor, particularly for residents of subdivisions or closely built lots in the interface, is the sense of cooperation as opposed to isolation in undertaking those measures that have mutual impacts. For instance, the presence of a significant number of vacant, untended lots containing extensive overgrown vegetation may produce a feeling among neighboring homeowners that their own efforts are worthless. Why bother?, they might ask, if it is clear the community is riddled with free riders who are failing to respond to the call to clear the area of fire-prone vegetation or to remove highly flammable substances from exposure to wildfires. Communities can counteract these perceptions through aggressive and visible enforcement efforts against absentee or irresponsible landowners.

That, in turn, leads to another critical factor in establishing any program that requires ongoing landowner cooperation. The officials involved, whether they are planners, fire personnel, foresters, or others, must establish an atmosphere of trust for the validity and efficacy of their programs through direct contact with the affected communities. Part of this involves listening to the actual concerns and perceptions of the community members, in part to learn what concerns and values drive their behavior in order to structure the message behind mitigation initiatives appropriately. Regulation within the WUI, other than addressing specific issues related to wildfire, is in many ways little different from many other zoning and building code enforcement efforts: Citizen cooperation invariably minimizes the amount of direct supervision required of the limited number of public personnel committed to the task.

However, as with many other hazard-reduction initiatives, wildfire involves some opportunity for those planning and implementing mitigation to reshape the message to convey the idea some measures actually produce additional benefits beyond risk reduction itself. In related hazard fields like floodplain management, this is known as multiple-objective management (Wetmore 1996)—the idea being, for instance, floodplain clearance can be combined with creating a greenway for recreational purposes. Researchers and foresters have reported people often respond more readily to the idea of "healthy forests" than to risk reduction, but clearing dead trees, reducing pest infestations, and other measures to reduce wildfire hazards can also qualify as restoring healthy forests. It is small surprise the title of the federal legislation supporting such efforts is Healthy Forests Restoration Act; the label had clearly acquired political cachet. Others have noted the effectiveness of selling homeowners on the benefits to some wildlife of efforts to clear overgrown vegetation, such as "quail like open habitat" (Nelson et al. 2002). The effectiveness of any particular message will most likely depend on local perceptions and influences, but the bottom line is experience has shown considerable latitude for such

A crucial factor, particularly for residents of subdivisions or closely built lots in the interface, is the sense of cooperation as opposed to isolation in undertaking those measures that have mutual impacts.

creativity in altering any number of behaviors that affect risk reduction with respect to wildfires. FEMA (2004) has provided a useful set of case studies in this regard.

INSTITUTIONAL AND LEGAL/POLITICAL BARRIERS

Those interviewed by APA during the course of the preparation of this report cited a number of existing institutional and legal/political barriers that impede effective planning responses to wildfires. While the severity of those barriers varies, depending on the section of the country and the complexity of intergovernmental relationships, the following are the most frequently cited.

- "Capacity of planning institutions, including enforcement; counties wary of using statutory authority" (Muller 2004).

- "Classic problem that some communities are in favor of growth, regardless. Oftentimes you butt up against the 'growth at any cost attitude'" (Rousch 2004).

- "Planning boards are not sufficiently aware that they can't change the environment to make it safe. . . . They're not accepting scientific facts about the nature of fires, and they're trying to defend undefendable development" (K. Stewart 2004).

- "The [federal] Clean Air Act and regulations are an impediment to safe, timely, and effective prescribed burns. They're killing any opportunity to do prescribed burn or slash pile burning. The U.S. Forest Service's hands are tied—they need to get rid of fuel, but they can't" (Worley 2004).

- "State laws regarding prescribed burns. In my state [Mississippi], prescribed burns are allowed by law for land management. In other states, the law is written to protect against fire, not to use fire. If I do a prescribed burn here, and someone is harmed, I am only civilly responsible [as opposed to criminally responsible]" (Brzuszek 2004).

- "Local councils are unwilling to adopt more stringent codes. They also don't have the funding or don't want to provide the funding to pay for fuel thinning" (Carpenter 2004).

- "The upfront costs of mitigation and risk assessments. These costs need to be part of the internal rate of return for a new development or an investor to factor in" (Topping 2004).

- "There is no reinsurance program to cover the losses of insurance companies. There needs to be a public/private program similar to the [National Flood Insurance Program]" (Topping 2004).

- "Making regulations that limit development in the high hazard areas. . . . People don't like regulations and, as a result, counties may be reluctant to make regulations for limiting development" (Garrison 2004).

- "There's a perception that it's someone else's responsibility to deal with wildfires. There is no profit in fire prevention. That's the biggest impediment: there's big money in putting up houses even if they will burn down a few years later, and no money in not building. Politicians choose whether to allow development or not. They got a lot of pressure from the people who can make money, and no pressure not to. The economic incentives are all on one side" (Weller 2004).

Many people interviewed by APA cited "private property rights" as a factor but regarded it more as an attitude of developers who believe they

Those interviewed by APA during the course of the preparation of this report cited a number of existing institutional and legal/political barriers that impede effective planning responses to wildfires.

have a right to purchase property and develop it as they please without substantial government interference (Weller 2004), rather than as a particular legal issue. Of those interviewed, no one could substantiate why tough restrictions on the location and density of development in the WUI, as well as requirements for use of fire-resistant materials or the provision of defensible space could be an infringement on property rights. The major institutional barrier seemed to be a lack of political will. "Some communities mandate clearing of property," said one U.S. Forest Service researcher, Pam Jakes, "and if you don't pay they'll put a lien on your house. You have to have the political strength and willingness to take that on. It requires a heavy-handed approach, but it is especially good for areas with a lot of absentee landowners" (Jakes 2004).

THREE STRATEGIES FOR DEALING WITH DEVELOPMENT IN THE WILDLAND-URBAN INTERFACE

This report's position is that there is no single approach to dealing with wildfires. As one interviewee declared, "If you put all your resources into suppression activities, that's the least effective. It seems obvious, but the least effective is not spreading your resources" (Mills 2004). At least three strategies, listed below, are necessary to address the problems of wildfires in the WUI.

(1) Conduct Wildfire Planning in a Comprehensive Planning Context

Eventually, where the political will exists to confront such questions, local elected officials and citizens may well ask whether they should be permitting development in wildfire-prone locations in the first place, and, if so, what conditions they should be imposing on such development in order to minimize the risk *before* they create a need to persuade a whole new set of WUI residents of the need to cooperate in ongoing mitigation efforts. In addition, they must confront the ongoing threat of wildfires in already developed areas.

From the review of the literature and interviews, there are two essential requirements. First, the state government must make it clear to local governments that a systematic approach to wildfire planning is the only one that is acceptable. The best way to do this is to make a natural hazards

This Gyrotrac is removing heavy fuels in an undeveloped lot in the Palm Coast subdivision in Flagler County, Florida.

Florida Division of Forestry

element of a local comprehensive plan a required element as a statement of statewide policy. Appendix F of this report contains a model of such an element, developed for the American Planning Association's Growing Smart℠ project, which is intended to address all types of natural hazards. Not all areas of a state may need to have wildfire planning, depending on vegetation and climate, so the legislation needs to be carefully crafted so some local governments can opt out of preparation where there is a clear case for so doing.

Second, the state must make resources available, including manuals, administrative rules, and training that interpret the new state requirement and provide clarification and assistance for local government. Initially, state governments may find it necessary to provide financial assistance to local governments to prepare such elements, which would need to be updated or reexamined on a periodic basis as new information or new development trends surface.

What should a local plan for wildfires include? As described in Chapter 4 of this report, the emerging practice is to have four to five components.

- *A hazard assessment.* Areas of the local jurisdiction prone to wildfires are identified and, using a rating system, mapped and prioritized, which is now typically performed with a geographic information system. Most interviewees believe this component of the plan does not present a major technical challenge although there can sometimes be incompatibility of data developed by jurisdictions. As Jack Cohen (2004) of the U.S. Forest Service remarked, "There are no significant technical barriers to planning for wildfires. We don't need to predict what a fire will do in real time." Cohen suggested priorities should be assigned based on relative exposure: (1) who lives there and what level of population is there, (2) the probable worst-case intensity of a fire based on vegetation, and (3) the frequency of weather conditions that will produce the worst-case intensity of a fire.

- *A specific risk assessment.* As noted in Chapter 4, this is often called a "vulnerability assessment." Vulnerability, in the natural hazards field, is typically defined as "the level of exposure of human life and property to damage from natural hazards," in this case from wildfire (Schwab et al. 1998). This analysis for wildfire planning purposes focuses on smaller areas described in terms of defensible space around buildings, an evaluation of roofing materials, building proximity, water supply, street widths, and fire department's capacity to respond to calls in a timely manner. Plans reviewed by APA tended to produce narrative descriptions of the characteristics of these areas.

- *An institutional analysis.* A description of the institutions and actors involved in wildfire planning and fire response and recovery. A plan should document the resources and capacities—including their adequacy and any shortfalls—of emergency management groups, fire departments (including staffing and equipment), and any intergovernmental mutual aid pacts. If groups of local governments are preparing their own plans, then this component can be prepared for all of them.

- *An evacuation and shelter component.* Plans should include a description of how people can get out of wildfire-prone areas in an emergency and in the event evacuation will be difficult, a designation of fire-hardened facilities that can serve as shelter until help arrives. Problems with creating multiple access routes are almost uniquely a function of steep terrain. In flatter environments, such as Florida and Minnesota, it is almost inconceivable any development site in the interface could not

These Florida homes abut a state forest. The noncombustible roofs are a positive aspect, but the minimal separation of structures presents a mutual exposure problem. The lawns of small vegetation are another positive feature. However, the proximity to the state forest could expose the homes to firebrands, so vigilance is required in removing combustibles, such as leaves and pine needles, away from the houses, gutters, and eaves. The situation also points out the need for collaborative planning by all parties in areas around state or national forests.

James Smalley

afford a bare minimum of two routes in and out, and preferably more, all of them adequate for entry by fire trucks as well. Even there, however, access along those routes can be obstructed through a lack of proper management of vegetation. Narrow streets with overgrown vegetation not only can impede movement by emergency vehicles but can also serve to advance, rather than retard, the movement of the wildfire itself by failing to provide a fuel break, however modest that might be. Still, the logic of planning adequate access and evacuation routes remains valid because they will be needed anyway under most circumstances. But the immediate situation may demand strategies other than evacuation, which may place people in greater danger than if they shelter in place. Decisions concerning the wisdom of evacuation in a fire emergency are the responsibility of emergency management personnel, but planners can work toward designing effective shelter in homes and subdivisions through good fire-safe design. For instance, requiring new subdivisions to include fireproof shelters residents can reach in an emergency should be a primary option, particularly where harsh terrain may create special challenges in moving large numbers of residents to safer locations. These would serve the same basic purpose for fire-prone areas as tornado shelters in areas subject to violent storms. And just as homes in tornado-prone areas can include "safe rooms" hardened to high-wind standards, so too can such rooms in new homes in the interface be designed to protect the lives of residents in the event of a wildfire without the necessity of evacuation.

- *Coordination of comprehensive plan elements.* An examination of the relationship of lands in the WUI to land-use, community facilities, and transportation proposals in the other elements of the comprehensive plan to ensure there are no conflicts and the elements are mutually supportive. This particular component is the missing link in many of the wildfire plans reviewed by APA. For example, land-use designations of one to two acres in areas prone to wildfires are certainly going to cause conflicts. Similarly, transportation routings that do not allow multiple access points into and out of a developing area or are inadequate in width for emergency vehicles are another. If an area is to be designated for intensive development, then centralized water facilities must also be available that provide adequate water flow.

- *A set of goals and policies.* The goals of policies of plans in Chapter 4 may provide a good starting place for communities trying to draft new WUI regulations.

- *A program of implementation.* The implementation program will usually take the form of proposals for changes in existing regulations, acquisition of key parcels of land or easements, construction of new facilities or utilities (such as fire stations, emergency shelters, or water lines), programs of prescribed burning, maintenance of publicly owned land to reduce biomass, and programs of public information (described below).

Finally, while a specialized task force or committee may develop the plan, it is essential that the planning commission and residents review it after a public hearing to see how suggestions have been implemented in the plan and before the legislative body adopts it. For its maximum effectiveness, the plan cannot be the proprietary document of any local government department or agency, but must be seen as a policy guide that cuts across all local government operations.

(2) Conduct a program of regulation and enforcement that stresses continuous individual responsibility by homeowners and property owners

Chapter 4 of this report has identified a number of standard techniques that constitute good practices for programs of regulation and enforcement. These include:

- Subdivision regulations, or their equivalent in other codes, that establish minimum street width, grade, turnaround, and multiple access requirements

- Zoning regulations establishing wildfire overlay districts for high-risk areas identified by a comprehensive plan and either requiring the clustering of development, restrictions on development in areas of steep slope and flammable vegetation, or extremely large lot sizes (lot sizes greater than one acre)

- Building or fire codes that specify minimum levels of fire-resistant material and practices for new construction, sprinklers, water supply, fuel or vegetative management plans that identify areas of defensible space around structures, and delineation of dead or live vegetation that must be removed for development to commence. Using fire-resistant material and construction practices is critical. Wildfire research indicates homes in the WUI are far from being merely a neutral factor in the overall fuel load feeding an advancing wildfire. A home is not simply like another tree in the fire's path. Its fuel density—the amount of flammable material per cubic foot of space—is typically several times that of the surrounding wildlands. If it ignites, it adds dramatically to the power and spread of the fire. Within the interface, in fact, wildfire spreads primarily from home to home, rather than merely from vegetation to home, and each additional home exploding in combustion multiplies the risk every other home will also ignite, particularly in closely built subdivisions. Although fire-resistant construction is a wise idea anywhere within a community, the structural fire protection services afforded in an urban setting are usually sufficient to contain individual building fires before they spread from house to house. In the WUI, however, other factors are at work because the forest itself provides an initial source of ignition. Without the homes, the fire might ordinarily serve some natural purposes, but the homes and their residents—as well as any critical facilities supporting their presence—instead become the

For its maximum effectiveness, the plan cannot be the proprietary document of any local government department or agency, but must be seen as a policy guide that cuts across all local government operations.

driving concern in the effort to suppress the fire. Building materials generally have fire-resistive-rated assembly times. The National Fire Protection Association (NFPA) 1144 and other systems include fire-resistant ratings. The NFPA 1144 requirements vary from 20 minutes to two hours, with the higher ratings applied to the most vulnerable parts of the structure, overhanging buildings, and the lesser times to items such as glass windows and exterior doors, exterior vertical walls, or skirts protecting open space beneath mobile and manufactured homes.

- Site plan review of developments in the WUI (with input from fire officials), which may include components of subdivision, zoning, and building regulation

- Ordinances establishing ongoing fuel reduction and elimination requirements for all property in the WUI

- Periodic inspection of buildings and lands in the WUI by local enforcement personnel to ensure conditions either imposed by ordinance or permit are continually satisfied, with the ability to impose fines or charges for local government elimination of flammable dead or live vegetative material in the form of a lien or an assessment

This last component, a regular program of enforcement, is among the most critical, and it places responsibility on the homeowner and property owner. "The attitude that homeowners share in the responsibility is in its infancy," said Jack Cohen of the U.S. Forest Service. "People are beginning to recognize that the fire department is not the sole responsible party for fire issues. Under wildfire conditions, a fire department cannot be effective without the community's preparation" (Cohen 2004).

This report takes the position that, if development is going to be permitted in some form in the WUI, then such development should be licensed for continued reinspection rather than permitted to continue as of right. This particular regulatory approach takes into account the fact that the problems of wildfire involve changes in vegetation on site and the impacts of weather on the condition of the vegetation and the prospect for fire. This approach should be applied to both existing development where the buildings themselves may be constructed of non-fire-resistant materials and to new development with fire-resistant buildings and site plans reviewed for mitigation proposals.

This report takes the position that, if development is going to be permitted in some form in the WUI, then such development should be licensed for continued reinspection rather than permitted to continue as of right.

Mixed vegetation with conifer next to a combustible wooden deck overlooking the sloping hillside make this house vulnerable, especially with the unprotected space beneath that can become a collection area for dry leaves and pine needles. Large windows increase the exposure hazard from radiant heat and flames.

Figure 5-1. Braingate Firewise Community Plan

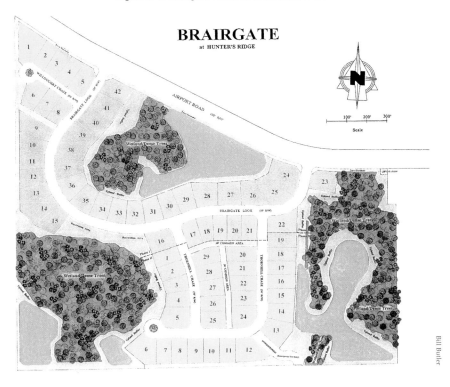

In this planned 2,300-home subdivision in Ormond Beach, Florida, the developer and landscape designer specify Firewise building and landscaping practices throughout the site, including fire-resistant building materials and defensible space around each house.

Bill Butler

This approach is commonly used in rental housing where local government reviews plans and conducts annual or biannual inspections to determine whether minimum standards of occupancy to safeguard residents are satisfied. If the criteria are met, a license is issued, which must be renewed periodically in order for the property to continue to be occupied. This approach treats development in the WUI more as a public health and safety issue and less as an issue of land-use control. Structured properly, with good cost analysis and management oversight, such a program can be established to pay for all or most of the costs involved in the initial review and continued site inspection. Key to the program would be the retention of records involved in the initial approval of a development. For example, an inspector looking at the conditions imposed at the time of permit issuance would be able to determine whether a property owner was still conforming with them. This particular approach has the benefit of continually putting the property owner on notice that prevention or mitigation of wildfire is an ongoing and personal duty, rather than one that is solely the duty of the government.

(3) Conduct an effective ongoing program of education and outreach to affected residents and property owners

In many ways, there are so many sources of experience to draw upon for crafting effective programs with respect to wildfire education that it ought not to be a daunting task. As with most other natural hazards, there are many stakeholders, both public and private, with some interest in both the structure and results of such a program. The main challenge lies in ensuring that everyone who should be involved has a meaningful role. In devising the following outline of an effective program, the authors are drawing both upon the well-established national Firewise Communities Program as well as upon the observations of knowledgeable people in the field. Those observations were gathered by APA both through the interviews conducted for this report and from the focus group interviews APA conducted previously in its evaluation of the Firewise training program (Schwab, Ross, and Walther 2003).

The recommendations relate mostly to the creation and maintenance of local education and outreach programs. That is where the real work now lies. Firewise Communities conducted a national series of workshops over four years, training more than 3,000 people. Those workshops were phased out in 2003, but the intent was to spawn state-level programs to continue it in shorter workshops reaching the local level. Some states like Florida have done a noteworthy job of extending this outreach to communities; others still need to fashion more aggressive programs. With or without such assistance, however, communities in the WUI need to craft local programs that maintain regular, ongoing contact with residents whose homes and properties are affected by wildfire hazards. The authors have identified the following five common, essential ingredients for an effective local program of education and outreach:

- Organize the program with both clear leadership and the widest possible involvement of stakeholders.

- Create an advisory committee comprising representation of the major stakeholders.

- To the extent possible, organize learning opportunities around hands-on activities.

- Assume residents can make intelligent choices and attempt to understand their perspectives on the wildfire problem.

- Establish clear priorities for focusing the message and content of any educational efforts.

The ability to recruit a wide variety of stakeholders and coordinate their involvement should drive the choice of leadership for a successful outreach program or leading a visioning process.

The ability to recruit a wide variety of stakeholders and coordinate their involvement should drive the choice of leadership for a successful outreach program or leading a visioning process. There is often a need to rise above specific agency agendas to foster effective participation and input from parties outside the lead agency, whether that is a fire, planning, or forestry department, or some other entity. In many communities, the key may lie with the qualifications of the program manager to facilitate effective citizen involvement as well as cooperation among local agencies, private organizations, and various levels of government. Colorado experts interviewed for this project, like members of a Colorado focus group for the Firewise evaluation, noted that county and municipal wildfire mitigation specialists have often proven effective in this role and may serve as a good model for communities elsewhere. Some of these officers maintain their own grant funds to assist homeowners with implementing desired changes on their properties (Garrison 2004; Johnson 2004).

This type of device, in the context of all-hazards recovery planning, was discussed at length in PAS Report 483/484, *Planning for Post-Disaster Recovery and Reconstruction* (Schwab et al. 1998). The sidebar includes some of the stakeholder groups suggested by Lincoln Walther (2004), who has worked as a consultant in the development of wildfire mitigation plans for several Florida communities, as well as by others. The strength of this approach is that it draws upon the resources of existing social and organizational networks rather than trying to invent new ones unless they are truly needed. Another good example of the enlistment of a broad array of stakeholders for such purposes is the statewide array of local FireSafe Councils in California, which list dozens of organizational supporters from the private sector.

POTENTIAL WILDFIRE MITIGATION ADVISORY COMMITTEE MEMBERS

- Planning department
- Public works department
- Fire department
- Water department
- County sheriff or police department
- Emergency services
- Chamber of commerce
- Homeowners associations
- City or county elected officials
- Planning commissioners
- Forest-related user groups (hunters, environmentalists, parks groups)
- Home repair suppliers (Lowe's, Home Depot, etc.)
- State and federal forestry and land management agencies
- Local building association
- Board of Realtors
- Insurance representatives

In working with these groups, it is important to maintain a positive focus and use whatever techniques are most effective locally. For example, Andre LeDuc (2004), an urban planning professor who leads a statewide hazards-related outreach program in Oregon under the aegis of the University of Oregon, has used community events like spaghetti dinners and a "commuter challenge" built around bicycling to incorporate elements of fun into a program he says can too easily focus on "gloom and doom," which turns people off. The best source for determining how to reach people will most likely be the target audience itself, the very reason for using

This diorama model of a WUI home is an easy way for agencies to demonstrate the concepts of Firewise to audiences at fairs and meetings. The defensible space, separation of vegetation, driveway to the main road, etc., are among aspects shown here. Firewise offers a heavy stock cutout version of a similar home with trees and outbuilding, and a guide for assembly and use. Ordering is done through the Firewise online catalog, free with postage.

James Smalley

advisory committees and similar devices to avoid a one-way stream of communication. For example, Web sites may seem like the latest, best tool, but if that is not how most people in a community get their information, its effectiveness may be close to nil.

At the local level, there is the greatest opportunity for direct, hands-on involvement. Many people interviewed for this project have noted the high value of directly involving residents in community wildfire mitigation activities, such as brush clearance days and demonstration projects, even though they must also maintain responsibility for mitigation on their own individual properties. The central idea is basically people learn more by doing than by simply listening or talking, and such strategies inevitably increase their ownership of the results.

In establishing community ownership of the program, it is also essential to understand and take advantage of the cultural factors in the community that will aid the success of the outreach program. Jack Cohen (2004), a USDA Forest Service researcher in Montana, noted that officials must approach interface residents with a desire to understand their perspective, not with condescension. Fire chiefs, he said, cannot afford simply to conclude, "Only idiots live out there," washing their hands of the problem. Instead, it is essential to educate residents about the trade-offs between the presence of various fuels and the use of specific building materials. Part of this process mentioned by several interviewees is the need to find within the affected neighborhoods a champion of the program and possibly a person or group willing to instigate an assessment of the problems they face. William Mills (2004), the wildfire mitigation official for Colorado Springs, Colorado, sums up the challenge as one of getting residents to "own the process and share the responsibility" for the program's effectiveness through the "systematic development of informed consent." Nan Johnson (2004), a planner with the Colorado State Forest Service, noted involvement can and should include residents outside the interface such as forest users from the city, who can learn regional water quality depends on forest management, and burning or cutting in the forest to manage fuel loads is "not always bad."

Finally, careful consideration must be given to the educational content of the program, based on local needs and priorities. Pam Jakes (2004), a Forest Service researcher in Minnesota, suggests, for instance, the use of demonstration homes and model sites can be an effective tool for removing some of the mystery from recommended mitigation techniques by letting people see how certain mitigation techniques really work. They can also demonstrate to observers that Firewise solutions can be aesthetically attractive. Ken Topping (2004), a California planning consultant, suggests the use of visioning and strategic planning as an involvement tool. Ultimately, this too is a matter for local creativity in connection with problems and priorities documented through the planning process. However, it is also an area where strong state programs, such as the one noted in Florida, can provide a good deal of ready-made content to keep local program managers from having to reinvent the wheel. This can be conveyed through state-sponsored brochures, videos, demonstration sites, and public service announcements.

Glossary of Terms

Unless otherwise noted, all definitions are drawn from the *Firewise Communities Participant Workbook*, 2nd Revised Edition, 2001, published by the Firewise Communities Program.

adaptive management. A systematic process for continually improving management policies and practices by learning from the outcomes of operational programs. Its most effective form—"active" adaptive management—employs management programs designed to experimentally compare selected policies or practices, by evaluating alternative hypotheses about the system being managed (British Columbia Ministry of Forests 2000).

aerial fuels. All live and dead vegetation in the forest canopy or above surface fuels, including tree branches, twigs and cones, snags, moss, and high brush (National Fire Plan 2004a).

biomass utilization. The harvest, sale, offer, trade, and/or utilization of woody biomass to produce the full range of wood products, including timber, engineered lumber, paper and pulp, furniture and value-added commodities, and bio-energy and/or bio-based products such as plastics, ethanol, and diesel (USDA, USDOE, and USDOI n.d.)

brush fire. A fire burning in vegetation that is predominantly shrubs, brush, and scrub growth.

canopy. The forest stratum containing the crowns of the tallest vegetation present (living or dead), usually above 20 feet.

Community Wildfire Protection Plan. In Title I of the Healthy Forests Restoration Act, a plan that:

- is developed in the context of the collaborative agreements and the guidance established by the Wildland Fire Leadership Council and agreed to by the applicable local government, local fire department, and state agency responsible for forest management, in consultation with interested parties and the federal land-management agencies managing land in the vicinity of the at-risk community;

- identifies areas for hazardous-fuel-reduction treatments, sets priorities for treating them, and recommends the types and methods of treatment on federal and nonfederal land that will protect one or more at-risk communities and their essential infrastructure; and

- recommends measures to reduce structural ignitability throughout the at-risk community (USDA and DOI 2004).

crown fire. A fire that advances from top to top of trees or shrubs more or less independent of a surface fire.

defensible space. An area, typically a width of 30 feet or more, between an improved property and a potential wildfire where the combustibles have been removed or modified.

duff. The layer of decomposing organic materials lying below the litter layer of freshly fallen twigs, needles, and leaves and immediately above the mineral soil.

firebreak. A natural or constructed barrier used to stop or check fires that may occur, or to provide a control line from which to work.

fire management plan. A strategic plan that defines a program to manage wildland and prescribed fires and documents the fire management program in the approved land-use plan. The plan is supplemented by operational plans such as preparedness plans, preplanned dispatch plans, prescribed fire plans, and prevention plans (USDA, USDOE, and USDOI n.d.)

fire regime. Periodicity and pattern of naturally occurring fires in a particular area or vegetative type, described in terms of frequency, biological severity, and area extent. For example, frequent, low-intensity surface fires with one- to 25-year return intervals occur in the southern pine forests of the southeastern United States, the saw grass everglades of Florida, the mixed conifer forests of the western Sierras of California, and so forth.

firebrand. Any source of heat, natural or human-made, capable of igniting wildland fuels. Flaming or glowing fuel particles that can be carried naturally by wind, convection currents, or by gravity into unburned fuels. Examples include leaves, pinecones, glowing charcoal, and sparks.

fire-resistive rating. The time that the material or construction will withstand fire exposure as determined by a fire test made in conformity with the standard methods of fire tests of building, construction, and materials.

Firewise construction. The use of materials and systems in the design and construction of a building or structure to safeguard against the spread of fire within a building or structure and the spread of fire to or from buildings or structures to the wildland/urban interface area.

Firewise landscaping. Vegetative management that removes flammable fuels from around a structure to reduce exposure to radiant heat. The flammable fuels may be replaced with green lawn, gardens, certain individually spaced green, ornamental shrubs, individually spaced and pruned trees, decorative stone, or other nonflammable or flame-resistant materials.

fuel management. A regular program of fuel modification.

fuel modification. Any manipulation or removal of fuels to reduce the likelihood of ignition or the resistance to fire control.

fuel treatment. A fuel treatment is any management operation implemented to reduce forest fuel accumulation. The principal goals of fuel treatments are to reduce fire line intensities, reduce the potential for crown fires, improve opportunities for successful fire suppression, and improve forest resilience to forest fires. Fuel treatments typically target canopy, ladder, and surface fuels to modify vegetation in each stratum. Thinning and prescribed fire target different components of the fuel bed of a given forest stand or landscape.

ground fire. A fire at ground level involving such combustible materials as grass, duff, loose surface litter, tree or shrub roots, rotting wood, leaves, peat, or sawdust.

interface. An area where wildland and housing meet (USDA and U.S. Department of the Interior 2001)

intermix. An area where wildland and housing intermingle (USDA and U.S. Department of the Interior 2001)

ladder fuels. Fuels that provide vertical continuity allowing fire to carry from surface fuels into the crowns of trees or shrubs with relative ease.

mitigation. Action that moderates the severity of a fire hazard or risk.

National Fire Plan (NFP). A plan developed in August 2000, following a landmark wildland fire season, with the intent of actively responding to severe wildland fires and their impacts to communities while ensuring sufficient firefighting capacity for the future. The NFP addresses five key points: firefighting, rehabilitation, hazardous fuels reduction, community assistance, and accountability. (National Fire Plan 2004b).

one-hour fuels. Fuels whose moisture content reaches equilibrium with the surrounding atmosphere within one hour. Fuels may be referred to as one-hour fuels, 10-hour fuels, etc., depending on their tendency to dry. (Private Forest Management Team n.d.)

overstory. That portion of the trees in a forest that forms the upper or uppermost layer.

prescribed burning. Controlled application of fire to wildland fuels in either their natural or modified state, under specified environmental conditions, which allows the fire to be confined to a predetermined area, and to produce the fire behavior and fire characteristics required to attain planned fire treatment and resource management objectives.

prescribed fire. A fire burning within prescription. This fire may result from either planned or unplanned ignitions.

understory. Low-growing vegetation (herbaceous, brush, or reproduction) growing under a stand of trees. Also, that portion of trees in a forest stand below the overstory.

wildfire. An unplanned and uncontrolled fire spreading through vegetative fuels, at times involving structures.

wildland. An area in which development is essentially nonexistent, except for roads, railroads, power lines, and similar transportation facilities. Structures, if any, are widely scattered.

wildland fire. Any fire occurring on the wildlands, regardless of ignition source, damages, or benefits.

wildland-urban interface (WUI). Any area where wildland fuels threaten to ignite combustible homes and structures.

List of References and Contacts

Alexander, M. E. 1982. "Calculating and Interpreting Forest Fire Intensities." *Canadian Journal of Botany* 60: 349–57.

Ashland, Oregon, City of. 2004. *Community Wildfire Protection Plan: Living with Fire in Ashland.*

Barkley, Yvonne Carree, Chris Schnepf, and W. Michael Colt. 2001. *Landscaping for Wildfire Prevention: Protecting Homes on the Wildland/Urban Interface.* Moscow: University of Idaho Cooperative Extension System.

Bielling, Jeff. 2004. Telephone interview with James Schwab, June 28.

British Columbia Ministry of Forests. 2000. "Definitions of Adaptive Management." [Accessed February 10, 2005]. Available at www.for.gov.bc.ca/hfp/amhome/amdefs.htm.

California Department of Insurance. 2004. "California FAIR Plan." [Accessed August 16, 2004]. Available at www.insurance.ca.gov/EXECUTIVE/FAIR Plan/CaliforniaFAIRPlan.htm.

California FAIR Plan. 2004. "Fair Access to Insurance Requirements." [Accessed August 16, 2004]. Available at www.cfpnet.com/.

California Governor's Office of Planning and Research. 2003. *Fire Hazard Planning.* Sacramento.

Clark County, Washington. 2004. *Wildland Urban Interface/Intermix Ordinance.* Chapter 15.13 of Title 15: Fire Prevention.

Cohen, Jack D. 1999. "Reducing the Wildland Fire Threat to Homes: Where and How Much?" [Accessed December 1, 2004]. Available at www.firelab.org/fbp/fbppubs/fbppdf/cohen/reducingwlfire.pdf.

Cohen, Jack D., and Bret W. Butler. 1998. "Modeling Potential Structure Ignitions from Flame Radiation Exposure with Implications for Wildland/Urban Interface Fire Management." Paper presented at the 13th Fire and Forest Meteorology Conference, Lorne, Australia.

Cohen, Jack, Nan Johnson, and Lincoln Walther. 2001. "Saving Homes from Wildfires: Regulating the Home Ignition Zone." *Zoning News*, May, 1–5.

Cova, Thomas. 2004. *Plenary #2: From the Ashes of the 2003 California Wildfires: Perspectives on the Future.* Presentation at the 29th Annual Workshop on Hazards Research and Applications, Boulder, Colorado, July 13.

Cronon, William. 1992. *Nature's Metropolis: Chicago and the Great American West.* New York: W.W. Norton & Co.

Dennis, F.C. "Creating Wildfire-Defensible Zones." Colorado State University Extension Fact Sheet 6–302, website [accessed June 30, 2004]. www.ext.colostate.edu/pubs/natres/06302.html.

Dwyer, John, et al. 2003. Mapping the Wildland Urban Interface and Projecting Its Growth to 2030: Summary Statistics. August. Evanston, Ill.: USDA Forest Service, North Central Research Station. [Accessed February 10, 2005]. Power Point presentation available at http://dnr.wi.us/org/land/forestry/fire/agenda/pdf/map_wuisecured.pdf.

Farquhar, Brodie. 2003. "Fire-prone properties could lose coverage." *Star-Tribune* (Casper, WY), March 24,. [Accessed August 2, 2004]. Available at www.casperstartribune.net/ articles/2003/05/21/news/c317f0d8a58d18887448966a1db71362.txt.

Federal Emergency Management Agency (FEMA). 2004. *At Home in the Woods: Lessons Learned in the Wildland/Urban Interface.* Washington, D.C.: FEMA. [Accessed December 1, 2004]. Available at www.fema.gov/regions/viii/athome_woods.shtm.

Florida, State of, Department of Community Affairs, and Florida Department of Agriculture and Consumer Services. 2004. *Wildfire Mitigation in Florida: Land Use Planning Strategies and Best Development Practices.* Tallahassee: Florida Department of Community Affairs.

Gage, Dennis. 2004. Manager, Insurance Services Office, Jersey City, N.J. Telephone interview with authors, August 16.

Gess, Denise, and William Lutz. 2002. *Firestorm at Peshtigo: A Town, Its People, and the Deadliest Fire in American History.* New York: Henry Holt & Co.

Glendale, California, City of, Planning Division. 2003. *Safety Element of the General Plan.*

Governor's Blue Ribbon Fire Commission. 2004. *Report to the Governor.* Sacramento: State of California.

Greater Flagstaff Forests Partnership (GFFP), and Ponderosa Fire Advisory Council (PFAC). 2004. *Community Wildfire Protection Plan for Flagstaff and Surrounding Communities in the Coconino and Kaibab National Forests of Coconino County, Arizona.* October 1.

Harrell, James. 2004. E-mail communication with James Schwab, June 29.

Hayward, City of, Department of Community and Economic Development. 1993. *City of Hayward Hillside Design and Urban/Wildland Interface Guidelines.* Resolution 93–037.

Hilbert, Emily. 2002. "Wildfires igniting more home insurance claims in West." [Accessed October 26, 2004]. Available at http://info.insure.com/home/wildfireclaims702.html.

Insurance Services Office (ISO). 2004. *Fireline: Pinpointing Insured Losses in the Southern California Wildfires of 2003.* [Accessed August 13, 2004]. Available at www.iso.com/ downloads/CA_Fire.pdf.

International Code Council. 2003. *International Urban-Wildland Interface Code.* Country Club Hills, IL.

Jefferson County, Colorado. 2002. *Section 49: Wildfire Hazard Overlay District.*

Johnson, Kenneth, and Calvin L. Beale. 2002. "Nonmetro Recreation Counties: Their Identification and Rapid Growth." *Rural America* 17, no. 4: 12–19.

———. 1998. "The Rural Rebound." *Wilson Quarterly* 12 (Spring): 16–27.

Johnson, Marie-Annette (Nan). 2004. E-mail communication with authors, September 28.

———. 2000. "The Los Alamos Cerro Grande Fire: An Abject, Object Lesson." *Natural Hazards Observer* 25, no. 1(September): 1–2.

Keeley, Jon. 2002. "Fire Management of California Shrubland Landscapes." *Environmental Management* 29, no. 3: 395–408.

Kickingbird, Kirke, and Karen Ducheneaux. 1973. *One Hundred Million Acres.* New York: McMillan Publishing Co.

McCaffrey, Sarah. 2004. "Thinking of Wildfire as a Natural Hazard." *Society and Natural Resources* 17: 509–516.

Mileti, Dennis, Sarah Nathe, Paula Gori, Marjorie Greene, and Elizabeth Lemersal. 2004. "Public Hazards Communication and Education: The State of the Art." [Accessed November 16, 2004]. Available at www.colorado.edu/hazards/informer/informerupdate.pdf.

Miller, Michael. 2003. "Snow, Rain Help Control California Wildfires." [Accessed February 10, 2005]. Available at www.planetark.com/dailynewsstory.cfm?/newsid=22733&newsdate=03-Nov-2003.

Montague, Ron. 2004a. E-mail communication with authors via Michele Steinberg, September 24.

———. 2004b. Telephone interview with Jim Schwab, November 3.

Murphy, Dean E. 2003. "In California's Inferno, an Oasis of Fire Safety Planning Stands Out." *New York Times*, November 2, National section, p. 20.

National Academy of Public Administration (NAPA). 2004. *Containing Wildland Fire Costs: Enhancing Hazard Mitigation Capacity*. Washington, D.C.: NAPA.

———. 2002a. *Wildfire Suppression: Strategies for Containing Costs*. Washington, D.C.: NAPA.

———. 2002b. *Wildfire Suppression: Strategies for Containing Costs: Background and Research*. Washington, D.C.: NAPA.

National Fire Plan. 2004a. Glossary. [Accessed February 10, 2005]. Available at www.fireplan.gov/resources/glossary/a.html.

———. 2004b. "What is the NFP?" [Accessed February 10, 2005]. Available at www.fireplan.gov/overview/whatis.html.

National Fire Protection Association (NFPA). 2002. *Standard for Protection of Life and Property from Wildfire*. NFPA 1144. Quincy, Mass.: NFPA.

National Interagency Fire Center (NIFC), Fire Investigation Team. 2000. *Cerro Grande Prescribed Fire, May 4–8, 2000: Investigation Report*. Boise, Idaho: NIFC.

Nelson, Kristen C., Martha C. Monroe, Jayne Fingerman Johnson, and Alison W. Bowers. 2002. "Public Perceptions of Defensible Space and Landscape Values in Minnesota and Florida." In *Homeowners, Communities, and Wildfire: Science Findings from the National Fire Plan*, compiled by Pamela J. Jakes. St. Paul, Minn.: USDA Forest Service, North Central Research Station.

Okeechobee County Technical Advisory Committee. 2003. *Okeechobee County Wildland Fire Mitigation Plan: A Countywide Approach*. Okeechobee, Fla.: Okeechobee County Fire Rescue.

Pinetop-Lakeside, Arizona, City of. 2003. *Forest Health and Fire Protection*. Chapter 16.117.

Prescott, Arizona, City of. 2003. *Urban-Wildland Interface Code*. Ordinance 4223. Section 6–2–2 of the city code. [Accessed January 3, 2005.] http://fire.cityofprescott.net/pdf/ord4223Wildland.pdf. Amended by Ordinance 4367. [Accessed January 5, 2005.] http://fire.cityofprescott.net/pdf/ord4367IUWIC.pdf.

Private Forest Management Team. n.d. Glossary. [Accessed November 10, 2004]. Available at www.pfmt.org/fire.

Pyne, Stephen J. 2004. Telephone interview with James Schwab, June 14.

———. 2001. *Fire: A Brief History*. Seattle: University of Washington Press.

———. 1982. *Fire in America: A Cultural History of Wildland and Rural Fire*. Seattle: University of Washington Press.

Pyne, Stephen J., Patricia L. Andrew, and Richard D. Laven. 1996. *Introduction to Wildland Fire.* 2nd ed. New York: John Wiley & Sons.

Rehm, Ronald G., Anthony Hamins, Howard R. Baum, Kevin B. McGrattan, and David D. Evans. 2002. "Community-Scale Fire Spread." NISTIR 6891.[Accessed December 1, 2004]. Available at http:fire.nist.gov/bfrlpubs/fire02/PDF/f02019.pdf.

Sandoz, Mari. 1992. *Hostiles and Friendlies: Selected Short Writings of Mari Sandoz.* Lincoln: University of Nebraska Press.

Santa Barbara, City of. 2003. *Proposed Wildland Fire Plan.*

Schwab, Jim. 2002. "Summary of State Land-Use Planning Laws." [Accessed December 1, 2004]. Available at http://www.ibhs.org/publications/view.asp?id=302.

Schwab, Jim, with Lynn Ross and Lincoln Walther. 2003. *Firewise Post-Workshop Assessment.* Chicago: APA for Firewise Communities.

Final Report. Chicago: APA for Firewise Communities.

Schwab, Jim, with Kenneth C. Topping, Charles D. Eadie, Robert E. Deyle, and Richard A. Smith. 1998. *Planning for Post-Disaster Recovery and Reconstruction.* Planning Advisory Service Report No. 483/484. Chicago: American Planning Association.

Sellers, Stephen. 2004. Plenary #2: From the Ashes of the 2003 California Wildfires: Perspectives on the Future. Presentation at the 29th Annual Workshop on Hazards Research and Applications, Boulder, Colorado, July 13.

Stewart, Susan I. 2004. E-mail communication with Jim Schwab, October 28.

Stewart, Susan I., Volker C. Radeloff, and Roger B. Hammer. 2003. "Characteristics and Location of the Wildland-Urban Interface in the United States." [Accessed December 1, 2004]. Available at http://silvis.forest.wisc.edu/Publications/PDFs Stewart_etal_2003.pdf.

Teie, William C., and Brian F. Weatherford. 2000. *Fire in the West: The Wildland/Urban Interface Fire Problem.* A Report for the Council of Western State Foresters. Rescue, Calif.: Deer Valley Press.

U.S. Census Bureau. 2001. "Population Change and Distribution: Census 2000 Brief." Washington, D.C.: U.S. Census Bureau. April.

U.S. Department of Agriculture, U.S. Department of Energy, and U.S. Department of the Interior. n.d. Memorandum of Understanding on Policy Principles for Woody Biomass Utilization for Restoration and Fuel Treatments on Forests, Woodlands, and Rangelands. [Accessed February 10, 2005]. Available at www.fireplan.gov/reports/404-418-en.pdf.

U.S. Department of Agriculture (USDA), and U.S. Department of the Interior (DOI). 2001. "Urban Wildland Interface Communities Within the Vicinity of Federal Lands That Are at High Risk from Wildfire." *Federal Register* 66, no. 3(January 4): 751–777.

U.S. Department of Agriculture (USDA) Forest Service. n.d. *National Wildfire Programs Database.* [Accessed January 3, 2005.] www.wildfireprograms.usda.gov/

U.S. Department of Agriculture (USDA) Forest Service and U.S. Department of the Interior (DOI), Bureau of Land Management (BLM). 2004. *The Healthy Forests Initiative and Healthy Forests Restoration Act: Interim Field Guide.* Washington, D.C.: USDA.

Vasievich, Mike. 1999. "Here Comes the Neighborhood! A New Gold Rush and Eleven Other Trends Affecting the Midwest." *NC News* (North Central Forest Experiment Station), August/September, 1–3.

Virginia Firewise Landscaping Task Force. 1998. *Virginia Firescapes Firewise Landscaping for Woodland Homes.* Blacksburg: Virginia Cooperative Extension.

Vogt, Christine. 2002. "Seasonal and Permanent Home Owners' Past Experiences and Approval of Fuels Reduction." In *Homeowners, Communities, and Wildfire: Science Findings from the National Fire Plan*, compiled by Pamela J. Jakes. St. Paul, Minn.: USDA Forest Service, North Central Research Station.

Vogt, Christine, Greg Winter, and Jeremy Fried. 2002. "Antecedents to Attitudes Toward Prescribed Burning, Mechanical Thinning, and Defensible Space Fuel Reduction Techniques." In *Homeowners, Communities, and Wildfire: Science Findings from the National Fire Plan*, compiled by Pamela J. Jakes. St. Paul, Minn.: USDA Forest Service, North Central Research Station.

Washington State Department of Community, Trade and Economic Development. 1999. *Optional Comprehensive Plan Element for Natural Hazard Reduction*. Olympia: State of Washington. June.

Watson, George, and Guy McCarthy. 2004. "Taking a Gamble and Living Among Nature," *San Bernardino Sun*, June 27.

Wetmore, French. 1996. *Reducing Flood Losses Through Multi-Objective Management*. Madison, Wis.: Association of State Floodplain Managers.

Whelan, Robert J. 1995. *The Ecology of Fire*. Cambridge, UK: Cambridge University Press.

Wilderness Society, The. 2003. "Summary of the Hayman Fire, Colorado." [Accessed October 26, 2004]. Available at http:www.wilderness.org/Library/Documents/WildfireSummary_Hayman.cfm.

Yakima County, Washington. 2001. *Urban-Wildland Interface Code*. Yakima County Ordinance [4–2001].

Formatted Interviews Conducted for This Project

The authors developed an eight-question survey tool that sought to elicit responses from a number of identified experts in various aspects of the subject of wildfire mitigation and planning. This list identifies the participants in those interviews, their titles and affiliations, and the date of each interview. Two participants (Carpenter and Glick) were interviewed together in a single telephone call. All interviews were conducted in 2004.

Batcher, Michael. Ecologist and Environmental Planner, Buskirk, New York. April 13.

Brzusek, Robert. Professor, Landscape Architecture, Mississippi State University. May 20.

Carpenter, Kelly. Director, Planning and Development, City of Denton, Texas. April 22.

Carpenter, Randy. Land-Use Planner, Sonoran Institute, Bozeman, Montana. April 20.

Cohen, Jack. Research Physical Scientist, U.S. Forest Service, Missoula, Montana. April 6.

Garrison, Kristin. Colorado State University.

Glick, Dennis. Director, Northwest Office, Sonoran Institute, Bozeman, Montana. April 20.

Hamling, David. President, Perry Park Metro District, Perry Park, Colorado. May 6.

Jakes, Pamela J. Research Project Leader, North Central Research Station, U.S. Forest Service, Minneapolis, Minnesota. May 18.

Johnson, Nan. Communities/Counties Coordinator, Planner, Colorado State Forest Service. April 15.

Le Duc, Andre. Professor, Urban and Regional Planning, University of Oregon, and Director, Oregon Natural Hazards Workshop, Eugene, Oregon. May 17.

Mills, William. Wildland Risk Management Officer, City of Colorado Springs, Colorado. May 20.

Muller, Brian. Assistant Professor, Urban and Regional Planning, University of Colorado at Denver. May 8.

Rousch, Joe. Urban Forester, City of Olympia, Washington. May 13.

Stewart, Kay. Landscape Architect, California. May 14.

Topping, Kenneth C. Principal, Topping Associates, Cambria, California. May 18.

Walther, Lincoln. Senior Urban and Regional Planner, Continental Shelf Associates, Jupiter, Florida. June 3.

Weller, Timber. Wildfire Mitigation Specialist, Florida Department of Agriculture, Division of Forestry. April 13.

Woods, Scott. Wildfire Mitigation Coordinator, Colorado State Forest Service. May 25.

Worley, Keith. Co-Chair, Perry Park FireWise Committee, Perry Park Metro District, Perry Park, Colorado. April 22.

Bibliography

Abt, R. C., M Kuypers, and J. B. Whitson. 1990. *A Case Study of Wildfire Mitigation Strategies in Wildland/Urban Development*. United States Department of Agriculture Forest Service, Federal Emergency Management Agency.

Alachua County, Florida. 2003. *Conservation and Open Space Element Revisions for Settlement*.

Amec. 2003. *Northeast Colorado Emergency Managers Association Hazard Mitigation Plan*.

Archuleta County. 2002. *Archuleta County Community Fire Plan: A Component of the National Fire Plan*. [Accessed: November 23, 2004]. Available at www.southwestcoloradofires.org/prevention/pdf/ArchuletaCounty FirePlan.pdf.

Arrowood, Janet C. 2003. *Living With Wildfires: Prevention, Preparation, and Recovery*. Denver: Bradford Publishing Company.

> This is basically a guide to owners of property in the wildland-urban interface (WUI), with regard to prevention, preparation, evacuation, recovery, and insurance, with a final section on history and background. Because most of it is geared to individual homeowners, it provides only hints to planners of what might be effective on a larger scale and largely ignores the question of the wisdom of building in vulnerable locations in the first place. Only in the final section on history and background does the author begin to discuss these issues.

Ashland, Oregon, City of. 2004. *Community Wildfire Protection Plan: Living with Fire in Ashland*.

———. 1994. *Development Standards for Wildfire Lands*.

Barkley, Yvonne Carree, Chris Schnepf, and W. Michael Colt. 2001. *Landscaping for Wildfire Prevention: Protecting Homes on the Wildland/Urban Interface*. Moscow: University of Idaho Cooperative Extension System.

Berg, Emmett, and Bill Boyarsky. 2004. *Losing Ground: How Taxpayer Subsidies and Balkanized Governance Prop Up Home Building in Wildfire and Flood Zones*. Los Angeles: Center for Governmental Studies.

Bielling, Jeff. 2004. Telephone interview with James Schwab, June 28.

Boulder County. 1995. *Boulder County Comprehensive Plan, Natural Hazards*. Boulder, Colo.: Boulder County.

> This is an excerpt from the 1995 comprehensive plan for natural hazards, which includes geologic hazards, erosion, flooding, and wildfire.

Boulder County Land Use Department. 1982. *Boulder County Comprehensive Plan, Fire Protection*. Boulder, Colo.: Boulder County.

———. 2002. *Wildfire Mitigation*. Boulder, Colo.: Boulder County Land Use Department. [Accessed February 10, 2005]. Available at www.co.boulder. co.us/lu/wildfire.

Boulder County Wildfire Mitigation Group. 2001. *The WHIMS Manual*. Boulder, Colo.: Boulder County.

Butry, David T., John M. Pye, and Jeffrey P. Prestemon. 2002. *Prescribed Fire in the Interface: Separating the People From the Trees*. United States Department of Agriculture Forest Service, Southern Research Station, North Carolina.

California Community Fire Plan Workgroup. 2003. *Community Fire Plan Template Outline.*

This is a complete outline for the contents of a community fire plan. A "topic" column lists the issues to be addressed. A "description" column is a basic introduction to the topic. Finally, there is a "where to get information" column that directs the reader to state (California) and other sources of information, especially those available on the Internet. The description column approaches the topic with a series of questions. This template emphasizes citizen participation and affected public agency buy-in as essential components of the fire plan.

California Department of Insurance. 2004. "California FAIR Plan." [Accessed August 16, 2004]. Available at www.insurance.ca.gov/EXECUTIVE/FAIR Plan/California FAIRPlan.htm.

California FAIR Plan. 2004. "Fair Access to Insurance Requirements." [Accessed August 16, 2004]. Available at www.cfpnet.com/.

Clark County, Washington. 2004. *Wildland Urban Interface/Intermix Ordinance.* Chapter 15.13 of Title 15: Fire Prevention.

Coconino County Community Development Department. 2003. *Coconino County Comprehensive Plan, Public Safety Element.*

Cohen, Jack D. 1999. "Reducing the Wildland Fire Threat to Homes: Where and How Much?" [Accessed December 1, 2004]. Available at www.firelab.org/fbp/fbppubs/ fbppdf/cohen/reducingwlfire.pdf.

Cohen, Jack D., and Bret W. Butler. 1998. "Modeling Potential Structure Ignitions from Flame Radiation Exposure with Implications for Wildland/Urban Interface Fire Management." Paper presented at the 13th Fire and Forest Meteorology Conference, Lorne, Australia.

Cohen, Jack, Nan Johnson, and Lincoln Walther, AICP. 2001. "Saving Homes From Wildfires: Regulating the Home Ignition Zone." *Zoning News* May, 1–5.

This article provides examples of ways planners can control wildfire hazards. Such options include land-use and development codes, overlay zone districts, nonconformity standards, subdivision regulations, etc. The authors stress codes need to be appropriate for the locality, and not used "blindly" from place to place. Examples of strategies implemented to mitigate wildfire risk in various counties and cities are provided.

Coleman, Ronny J. 1994. *Urban-Wildland Fire Problem: The Policy Context.* Sacramento, Calif.: State Fire Marshal.

This document analyzes policy issues involved in the WUI, such as economic losses and the impact of jurisdictional boundaries on building codes and mitigation efforts. The document includes recommendations and a time line for improving mitigation strategies through positioning (government involvement at all levels), education, partnering, and enforcement.

Colorado Springs, City of 2001. *Comprehensive Plan: City of Colorado Springs.*

———. *Wildfire Risk Management.* [Accessed February 10, 2005]. Available at www.springsgov.com/Page.asp?NavID=1225.

Colorado Springs, City of, City Planning Group Development Review Unit. 1996. *City of Colorado Springs Hillside Development Design Manual.*

Colorado Springs Fire Department. 2001. *Colorado Springs Fire Department Wildfire Mitigation Plan 2001.*

Colorado State Forest Service. 1997. *Wildfire Hazard Mitigation and Response Plan.* Fort Collins: Colorado State University.

This is a clever fill-in-the-blanks plan for local governments. Part I covers general information about the area that is the subject of the plan including type of home construction, access, water supply, utilities, and evaluation of hazards. Part II contains potential mitigation actions by individual homeowners, subdivision homeowner associations, fire departments, the sheriff, and other agencies. Part III is a model response plan, which catalogues typical problems, expected fire behavior, alarm response responsibility, and an organization structure and management framework for responding to fires.

Cova, Thomas. 2004. Plenary #2: From the Ashes of the 2003 California Wildfires: Perspectives on the Future. Presentation at the 29th Annual Workshop on Hazards Research and Applications, Boulder, Colorado, July 13.

Cronon, William. 1992. *Nature's Metropolis: Chicago and the Great American West.* New York: W.W. Norton & Co.

de Jong, Lisa. 2002. *Improving Fire Hazard Assessment at the Urban-Wildland Interface: Case Study in South Lake Tahoe, CA.* Davis, Calif.: United States Department of Agriculture Forest Service, Pacific Southwest Research Station.

Dennis, Frank C. 2003. *Creating Wildfire-Defensible Zones.* Colorado State University Cooperative Extension.

This publication describes defensible space and how it can be achieved by using management zones. Tables, graphs, and drawings are provided to guide spacing of trees and to recommend plant types. An annual checklist for homeowners is also provided.

———. 2002. *Fire-Resistant Landscaping.* Colorado State University Cooperative Extension.

This is a short guide for homeowners to use when landscaping their property. Guidelines are provided regarding the placement, type, and maintenance of plants that are most fire resistant, particularly for Colorado.

———. 2000. "Planning for Wildfire Safety in Colorado's Wildland Urban Interface." *Land Development,* 12–17.

Denver Regional Council of Governments (DRCOG). 2003. *Denver Regional Natural Hazard Mitigation Plan.*

Department of Community and Economic Development. 1993. *City of Hayward Hillside Design and Urban/Wildland Interface Guidelines.*

The WUI guidelines contained in this report address building construction standards for fire protection, fuel modification, and management at the interface, as well as fire-resistant landscaping.

Division of Forest Resources, Natural Resources, and Community Development. 1985. *Fire Safety Considerations for Developments in Forested Areas: A Guide for Homeowners, Home Buyers, and Builders.*

Dolores County, Colorado. n.d. *Dolores County Community Fire Plan: A Component of the National Fire Plan.* [Accessed: November 23, 2004]. Available at www.southwestcoloradofires.org/prevention/pdf/DoloresCountyCommunity WildfirePlan.pdf.

Dubey, Manvendra. 2000. "Computer Model Assesses Wildfire Emission." *The Forestry Source* (2000). [Is this an article in a magazine or something else? Need complete reference information]

Dwyer, John, et al. 2003. Mapping the Wildland Urban Interface and Projecting Its Growth to 2030: Summary Statistics. August. Evanston, Ill.: USDA Forest Service, North Central Research Station. [Accessed February 10, 2005]. Power Point presentation available at http://dnr.wi.us/org/land/forestry/fire/agenda/pdf/map_wuisecured.pdf.

East Bay Municipal Utility District 1992. *Firescape: Landscaping to Reduce Fire Hazard.*

Ebarb, Pat. 1996. *Fire Protection in Rural America: A Progress Report.* Washington, D.C.: National Association of State Foresters.

Fairbanks, Frank, Allan V. Burman, Gail Christopher, Patrick J. Kelly, Lyle Laverty, Keith Mulrooney, Paul Posner, and Charles Wise. 2003. *Containing Wildland Fire Costs: Utilizing Local Firefighting Forces.* Washington, D.C.: National Academy of Public Administration.

Farnsworth, Allen, and Paul Summerfelt. 2001. *Flagstaff Interface Treatment Prescription: Results in the Wildland/Urban Interface.* Flagstaff, Ariz.: City of Flagstaff.

Farquhar, Brodie. 2003. "Fire-prone properties could lose coverage." *Star-Tribune* (Casper, WY), March 24,. [Accessed August 2, 2004]. Available at www.casperstartribune.net/articles/2003/05/21/news/c317f0d8a58d18887448966a1db71362.txt.

Federal Emergency Management Agency (FEMA). 2004. *At Home in the Woods: Lessons Learned in the Wildland/Urban Interface.* Washington, D.C.: FEMA. [Accessed December 1, 2004]. Available at www.fema.gov/regions/viii/athome_woods.shtm.

———. 2004. *Multi-Hazard Mitigation Planning Guidance under the Disaster Mitigation Act of 2000.* Washington, D.C.: FEMA.

———. 1992. *Report of the Operation Urban Wildfire Task Force.* Washington, D.C.: FEMA.

Good for historical perspective, this document highlights the findings of a 1992 panel on urban wildfires that resulted from the disastrous 1991 East Bay Hills wildfire in Oakland. Many of its findings point to problems that became common currency for Firewise efforts throughout the 1990s and beyond.

Fernandes, Paulo M., and Herminio S. Botelho. 2003. "A Review of Prescribed Burning Effectiveness in Fire Hazard Reduction." *International Journal of Wildland Fire,* June, 117–28.

Florida Department of Community Affairs, and Florida Department of Agriculture and Consumer Services. 2004. *Wildfire Mitigation in Florida: Land Use Planning Strategies and Best Development Practices.* Tallahassee: Florida Department of Community Affairs.

Forest Health Oversight Council. 2004. *The Report of the Governor's Arizona Forest Health Oversight Council: Draft for Public Consideration.* Executive Order 2003–16. Phoenix: State of Arizona.

This document was produced by the Forest Health Oversight Council of the State of Arizona to provide a brief assessment of Arizona's forests and wildfires and to provide recommendations for the health and safety of its future. There are thirty recommendations: ten that require legislative changes, fifteen for the governor and executive branch, four for funding and implementation of treatments, and one that pertains to landowners.

Frady, Steven R. 1992. *Wildfire Protection for Homeowners & Developers: A Guide to Building and Living Firesafe in the Wildlands.* Sierra Front Wildfire Cooperators, Nevada.

Gadsby, William J. et al. 2004. *Containing Wildfire Costs: Background Report.* Washington, D.C.: National Association of Public Administration.

———. 2004. *Containing Wildland Fire Costs: Enhancing Hazard Mitigation Capacity.* Washington, D.C.: National Academy of Public Administration.

Gage, Dennis. 2004. Manager, Insurance Services Office, Jersey City, New Jersey. Telephone interview with authors, August 16.

Gavin, Mike. 2003. *Northern Colorado Regional Hazards Mitigation Plan.* Fort Collins, Colo.: Fort Collins Office of Emergency Management.

Gess, Denise, and William Lutz. 2002. *Firestorm at Peshtigo: A Town, Its People and the Deadliest Fire in American History.* New York: Henry Holt and Company, LLC.

This book combines intriguing social history of Peshtigo, Wisconsin, in the mid-1800s with an impressive array of practical facts about the 1871 firestorm. The authors make very clear connections that most people are completely unaware of, such as why this fire occurred on the very same day as the Great Chicago Fire and for largely the same sorts of reasons, which were related to lumber industry practices of the times. This is a useful addition to the historical literature on U.S. wildfire experiences.

Glendale, California, City of, Planning Division. 2003. *Safety Element of the General Plan.*

Governor's Blue Ribbon Fire Commission. 2004. *Report to the Governor.* Sacramento: State of California.

Great Lakes Forest Fire Compact. 2002. *Protecting Life and Property From Wildfire: An Introduction to Designing Zoning & Building Standards for Local Officials.* [Accessed February 10, 2005]. Available at www.michigan.gov/dnr/0,1607,7-153-10367_11851-33529--,00.html.

This is a briefing paper for local officials on the basics of zoning and building standards for wildfires. Despite its short length, it covers a lot of ground, including landscaping to create a "defensible space" around buildings, vehicular access to provide for emergency equipment and civilian evacuation, and structural design and constructional considerations, in particular roofing.

Greater Flagstaff Forests Partnership (GFFP), and Ponderosa Fire Advisory Council (PFAC). 2004. *Community Wildfire Protection Plan for Flagstaff and Surrounding Communities in the Coconino and Kaibab National Forests of Coconino County AZ.* October 1.

Gunnison County Local Emergency Management Committee. 2003. *All-Hazard Local Mitigation Plan 2003.*

Harrell, James. 2004. E-mail communication with James Schwab, June 29.

Harrell, R. D. Dick, and William C. Teie. 2001. *Will Your Home Survive? A Winner or Loser?: A Guide to Help You Improve the Odds Against Wildland Fire.* Rescue, Calif.: Deer Valley Press.

A large portion of the text is devoted to discussing fuels and their impact on fire. There are four different types of fuels identified by the authors—grass, brush, timber litter, and slash—that are essentially the debris that remains after logging. Fuel terms and definitions are provided to further the reader's understanding of the variables to consider and what impact they have on fire behavior. Similar information is provided in regard to weather and topography.

Another section provides examples of eleven fuel models, with pictures to show what the fuel model looks like regularly and what it would look like if it were on fire. The first two fuel models consist of grasses, and the authors note: "Never underestimate the dangers associated with grass fires. They can easily overtake a person." Grasses represent a much higher risk than one might assume. Explanations and pictures are given for all four fuel types (grass, brush, timber litter, and slash), and a chart is shown comparing all characteristics of each of the eleven fire models.

Hawver, Chris, and Michael S. Batcher. 2002. *Fire Management Plan for the Albany Pine Bush Preserve.* Albany, N.Y.: Albany Pine Bush Preserve.

Hard-to-follow fire management plan for a 2000-acre area near Albany, New York. The overall objective of the plan appears to be to establish protocols for prescribed burning of a pitch-pine scrub oak barrens area that provides a habitat for the Karner blue butterfly. Plan contains a lengthy set of protocols for the conduct of prescribed fires, including weather and fire behavior parameters, fire crew qualifications and equipment, and guidelines for wildfire management.

Hermansen, L. Annie, and Edward A. Macie. 2002. *Human Influences on Forest Ecosystems.* General Technical Report SRS-55. United States Department of Agriculture Southern Research Station, North Carolina.

This report encompasses many topics related to the WUI, including population trends, economic issues, forest management, and social consequences. This is not a fire-specific document, but rather a thorough examination of problems encountered as development advances at the urban fringe. An example from Charleston, South Carolina, indicates the ratio of percentage increase in population to percentage increase in urban land is 1:6 from 1979 to 1999; during the same time period the population of Mobile, Alabama, grew 25 percent while the urban land use doubled.

The costs of converting wildland to residential land are discussed on the micro- and macroeconomic levels. The practice of *ad valorem* property tax is cited as a pressure on forest owners to sell their land for parcelization to developers. Municipalities also face pressure to acquire wildland to increase property tax revenues.

The report points out disaster loans that may encourage homeowners to build "inappropriate and high-risk construction" are one barrier to preventing development in the WUI. Prescribed burns are discussed as an option to promote forest health, but the Environmental Protection Agency's definition of smoke as an air pollutant can be a barrier to its use as well. Examples of alternative zoning ordinances are provided as ways to "protect forests, wetlands, floodplains, or environmentally sensitive lands," but not necessarily to prevent wildfires or development in the WUI.

Hilbert, Emily. 2002. "Wildfires igniting more home insurance claims in West." [Accessed October 26, 2004]. Available at http://info.insure.com/home/wildfireclaims702.html.

Hudson, Rachel, Pam Jakes, Erika Lang, and Kristen Nelson. 2003. *Berkeley Township, New Jersey.* United States Department of Agriculture Forest Service.

This is a case study about Berkeley Township, New Jersey. Berkeley Township has recently created a Fire Safe Committee to help educate citizens about their role in wildfire preparedness. Berkeley Township is a popular retirement destination and as a result has many senior citizens. In response to the added concerns of these residents, neighborhood associations have created a database of all required medications in case they are left behind during evacuation and have organized a pet trailer to rescue pets. Berkeley Township has also taken steps to coordinate among its three separate volunteer fire companies so they may work together in an emergency.

Inland Empire Society of American Foresters. 2001. *Fuel Management Can Reduce Wildfire Risks.* Society of American Foresters, Maryland.

Institute for Business & Home Safety (IBHS). 2001. *Is Your Home Protected From Wildfire Disaster?: A Homeowner's Guide to Wildfire Retrofit.* Tampa, Florida.

This publication is intended for individuals whose homes are located in the WUI. It provides information about the spread of wildfire, how a "zoned approach" to landscape can help protect a home, as well as building materials and design guidelines that can be used to help protect a home. Also included is a checklist to help ensure safety before, during, and after a wildfire.

Insurance Services Office (ISO). 2004. *Fireline: Pinpointing Insured Losses in the Southern California Wildfires of 2003.* [Accessed August 13, 2004]. Available at www.iso.com/downloads/CA_Fire.pdf/

International Code Council. 2003. *International Urban-Wildland Interface Code.* Country Club Hills, Ill.: International Code Council, 2003.

This model code establishes minimum regulations for land use and buildings in designated WUI areas using prescriptive and performance-related provisions. Under the model, the local legislative body declares certain areas to be WUI zones, which are then mapped. Permits are required for the construction of buildings or structures in such areas, unless there is a building or fire code with similar requirements. The code contains access, water supply, and fire protection planning requirements for the interface. Building code requirements contain a ranking system for hazard severity, based on slope and type of fuel, ignition-resistant construction, sprinkler systems, and defensible space. Appendices include a checklist for assessing fire hazard severity and a description of the different kinds of fuels that support wildfires.

Interviews Conducted for This Project. See Appendix B. List of References and Contacts.

Irwin, Bob. 1989. *A Discussion of the County General Plan and the Role of Strategic Fire Protection Planning.* Sacramento: California Department of Forestry and Fire Protection.

Jakes, Pam, Shurti Agrawal, and Martha Monroe. 2003. *The Palm Coast Community: Steps to Improve Community Preparedness for Wildfire.* United States Department of Agriculture Forest Service, North Central Research Station.

Palm Coast, Florida, developed in the early 1970s as a retirement community. As a result of a fire in 1985, a county ordinance was drafted that would help protect the area by reducing vegetation on undeveloped private lots. A revised ordinance has since passed that allows the city to clear vegetation if it is not done by the owner. Many other steps have been taken to prepare the city for wildfire including education; cooperation among state, county, and city government; and emergency communication strategies.

———. 2003. *Waldo, Florida: Steps to Improve Community Preparedness for Wildfire.* United States Department of Agriculture Forest Service, North Central Research Station.

Due to its small size and limited budget, Waldo has had to rely on partnerships with other nearby towns, the county, and the state in order to prepare for wildfire.

Jakes, Pam, and Kristen Nelson. 2002. *Gunflint Trail Community: Steps to Improve Community Preparedness for Wildfire.* United States Department of Agriculture Forest Service, North Central Research Station.

The Gunflint Trail in Minnesota is prone to wildfires, and residents have mobilized to keep their communities safe by being prepared. They have created partnerships with residents, business owners, and public agencies to share in the responsibility of wildfire preparedness. They have also made efforts to improve benefits for volunteer firefighters to help "professionalize" volunteer fire departments.

Jakes, Pam, and Victoria Sturtevant. 2002. *The Bend Community & FireFree: Steps to Improve Community Preparedness for Wildfire.* United States Department of Agriculture Forest Service, North Central Research Station.

Bend, Oregon, has experienced rapid growth and expansion into forested areas. As a result of devastating wildfires in 1990 and 1996, the SAFECO Insurance Company wanted to prevent future fires and gave money to the fire department to start a public education campaign called FireFree. FireFree has provided information to residents about defensible space, clearing vegetation around homes, and other ways to be prepared for a wildfire. FireFree has also partnered with local landfills to allow residents to recycle land debris at no cost once a year.

Jefferson County, Colorado. 2002. *Section 49: Wildfire Hazard Overlay District.*

Johnson, Kenneth, and Calvin L. Beale. 1998. "The Rural Rebound." *Wilson Quarterly* 12 (Spring): 16–27.

———. 2002. "Nonmetro Recreation Counties: Their Identification and Rapid Growth." *Rural America* 17, no. 4: 12–19.

Johnson, Marie-Annette (Nan). 2004. E-mail communication with authors, September 28.

———. 2000. "The Los Alamos Cerro Grande Fire: An Abject, Object Lesson." *Natural Hazards Observer* 25, no. 1(September): 1–2.

Josephine County, Oregon. 2003. *Article 76: Wildfire Safety Standards.*

Keeley, Jon. 2002. "Fire Management of California Shrubland Landscapes." *Environmental Management* 29, no. 3: 395–408.

Kickingbird, Kirke, and Karen Ducheneaux. 1973. *One Hundred Million Acres.* New York: McMillan Publishing Co.

Kootenai County, Idaho. 2003. *Ordinance No. 317.*

McCaffrey, Sarah. 2004. "Thinking of Wildfire as a Natural Hazard." *Society and Natural Resources* 17: 509–516.

Mileti, Dennis, Sarah Nathe, Paula Gori, Marjorie Greene, and Elizabeth Lemersal. 2004. "Public Hazards Communication and Education: The State of the Art." [Accessed November 16, 2004]. Available at www.colorado.edu/hazards/informer/ informerupdate.pdf.

Miller, Michael. 2003. "Snow, Rain Help Control California Wildfires." [Accessed February 10, 2005]. Available at www.planetark.com/dailynewsstory.cfm?/ newsid=22733&newsdate=03-Nov-2003.

Monroe, Martha L., Alison W. Bowers, and L. Annie Hermansen. 2003. *The Moving Edge: Perspectives on the Southern Wildland-Urban Interface.* United States Department of Agriculture Forest Service Southern Research Station, North Carolina.

The most fascinating aspect of this brief report is the variety of perspectives coming out of state-level focus groups within just one region of the United States. Many focus group comments are indicative of the fact this is very much a people problem, and many of the problems stem from popular perceptions and attitudes and less from our physical and scientific ability to anticipate problems.

Montague, Ron. 2004. E-mail communication with authors via Michele Steinberg, September 24.

———. 2004. Telephone interview with Jim Schwab, November 3.

Montana Department of Environmental Quality. 2003. *Example Burn Plan Addressing Air Resource Impacts From Prescribed Fire Smoke.* Montana Department of Environmental Quality.

Montana Department of Justice, Fire Prevention & Investigation, and Montana Department of State Lands, Fire Management. 1993. *Fire Protection Guidelines for Wildland Residential Interface Development.* Montana Department of State Lands.

Murphy, Dean E. 2003. "In California's Inferno, an Oasis of Fire Safety Planning Stands Out." *New York Times*, November 2, National section, p. 20.

National Academy of Public Administration (NAPA). 2004. *Containing Wildland Fire Costs: Enhancing Hazard Mitigation Capacity.* Washington, D.C.: NAPA.

For planners' purposes, this is the most useful document in the NAPA series, because it focuses on reducing wildfire losses through mitigation.

———. 2003. *Containing Wildland Fire Costs: Improving Equipment and Services Acquisition.* Washington, D.C.: National Academy of Public Administration.

———. 2002. *Wildfire Suppression: Strategies for Containing Costs.* Washington, D.C.: National Academy of Public Administration.

This report is part of an ongoing series of federally funded NAPA studies of wildfire policy and its budgetary implications. It begins by analyzing the varying circumstances and suppression costs of selected case study wildfires of recent vintage. The opening section ends with panel conclusions, leading off with the statement that "extreme buildups of hazardous fuels and drought conditions" are likely to cause some wildfires to grow too fast to allow timely suppression, thus escalating costs for suppressing a fire on a far wider scale. It also examines problems stemming from urban and developed areas near federal lands vulnerable to fires and how costs can and should be shared between such agencies. The study then moves on to a series of recommendations for more cost-effective firefighting and management in the future, followed by challenges to key stakeholders in the policy-making process.

———. 2002. *Wildfire Suppression: Strategies for Containing Costs: Background and Research.* Washington, D.C.: National Academy of Public Administration.

This largely consists of more detailed data supplements to the primary NAPA study on wildfire suppression and cost containment.

———. 2001. *Managing Wildland Fire: Enhancing Capacity to Implement the Federal Interagency Policy.* Washington, D.C.: National Academy of Public Administration.

National Fire Plan. 2001. *A Collaborative Approach for Reducing Wildland Fire Risks to Communities and the Environment.* Washington, D.C.: National Fire Plan.

———. 2001. *Managing the Impact of Wildfires on Communities and the Environment.* Washington, D.C.: USDA Forest Service and Department of the Interior.

National Fire Protection Association (NFPA). 2002. *Standard for Protection of Life and Property From Wildfire.* NFPA 1144. Quincy, Mass.: NFPA.

National Interagency Fire Center (NIFC), Fire Investigation Team. 2000. *Cerro Grande Prescribed Fire, May 4–8, 2000: Investigation Report.* Boise, Idaho: NIFC.

National Wildland/Urban Interface Fire Protection Program. 1998. *Wildland/Urban Interface Fire Hazard Assessment Methodology.* Washington, D.C.: National Wildland/ Urban Interface Fire Protection Program.

This document provides basic information about wildfire ignition and spread, as well as some building and vegetation prevention measures. It also provides an example of how to rank and visualize wildfire hazards using grids, matrices, and a geographic information system (GIS) in order to strategize for future fires.

Nelson, Kristen C., Martha C. Monroe, Jayne Fingerman Johnson, and Alison W. Bowers. 2002. "Public Perceptions of Defensible Space and Landscape Values in Minnesota and Florida." In *Homeowners, Communities, and Wildfire: Science Findings from the National Fire Plan,* compiled by Pamela J. Jakes. St. Paul, Minn.: USDA Forest Service, North Central Research Station.

North Port, Florida, City of. 2003. *Ordinance No. 86–206, Relating to the Maintenance of Properties and Premises.*

This ordinance, in Section 4, prohibits "excessive growth" of cultivated or uncultivated grass, weeds, or underbrush in excess of 12 inches. The ordinance provides that shrubs, trees, bushes, or other natural or cultivated species of foliage found and/or planted upon an occupied or unoccupied lot may not become a "fire or safety hazard to neighboring premises."

Northwest Interagency Fire Group. 1978. *Fire Safety Considerations for Developments in Forested Areas: A Guide for Planners and Developers.* Interagency Fire Prevention Group, Oregon.

Novato Fire Protection District Fire Loss Management Division. 2001. *Fire Protection Standard 220: Vegetation/Fuels Management Plan.* Novato, Calif.: City of Novato.

Nowicki, Brian. 2001. *Protecting Communities From Forest Fires: Effectively Treating the Wildland Urban Interface.* Flagstaff, Ariz.: Southwest Forest Alliance.

This document discusses the ways in which wildfires can be mitigated through defensible space and use of the "intensive zone" concept of defensible space. The "intensive zone" extends beyond defensible space, and its purpose is to "reduce the intensity of an approaching wildfire" by reducing it to a surface fire. The author states several times that wildfire mitigation should not seek to eliminate wildfire altogether or thin the forest in an extreme matter, but rather to protect homes and businesses through preventative measures, such as defensible space and vegetation management.

Office of Community Services, Fort Lewis College. 2002. *National Fire Plan: La Plata County Community Fire Plan.* Durango, Colo.: Fort Lewis College.

This plan stresses the use of a wildfire hazard assessment and maps of the county, available through the U.S. Forest Service. Interestingly, the mapping project shows that environments likely to produce the most damaging and uncontrollable fire behavior are those with steep southerly slopes and oak, ponderosa pine, or pinyon-juniper vegetation, which are the most popular places for new developments to occur. The plan identifies areas of "high risk and concern" with priorities set by different fire departments and districts.

Okeechobee County Technical Advisory Committee. 2003. *Okeechobee County Wildland Fire Mitigation Plan: A Countywide Approach.* Okechobee, Fla.: Okeechobee County Fire Rescue.

This is a countywide mitigation plan for Okeechobee County, Florida. The introductory portion of the plan lists the various groups involved in the creation of the plan who are critical to the structure of wildfire mitigation and who provide a direct link to local property owners. The next portion discusses various rating systems available to assess wildfire risk, and explains why the county chose a combination of two to be used. The actual assessment checklist is provided, including common things such as accessibility by rescue crews, and vegetation issues, but also including more unique items such as "helicopter dip spots" to ensure helicopter access. The assessment for the county was completed at the subdivision level since parcel level information would be too detailed for such a large area.

Recommendations are given for the county overall, including the implementation of Firewise and an increase in firefighting capabilities. Recommended actions are also provided for various county offices and services, including the Department of Planning and Development (whose Comprehensive Plan policies do not directly address wildland fire) and the School District (whose Emergency Plan does not directly address wildland fire threat or evacuation). A lengthy table shows what type of mitigation strategy would be appropriate for parcel and single structures, neighborhoods and subdivisions, and institutions. The table also indicates whether the strategy is applicable in Okeechobee County, what the cost would be, the level of feasibility, the level of public acceptance, and what the environmental consequences would be.

The next section provides a mitigation strategy with a table describing each project, the implementation methodology, the responsible leader, the auxiliary support, and a completion date. The document ends with an overall implementation program, similar to the mitigation strategy. The implementation program also makes recommendations for funding sources.

Orange County Wildland/Urban Interface Task Force Subcommittee on Open Space Management. 1997. *Wildland/Urban Interface Development Standards.* San Diego: San Diego County Fire Chiefs Association.

Oregon Department of Land Conservation and Development and Community Planning Workshop. 2000. *Planning for Natural Hazards: Comprehensive Plan Review.* Salem: Oregon Department of Land Conservation and Development.

This is an excellent series of documents, not just on planning for wildfires, including incorporating such goals in local comprehensive plans, but also planning for every major kind of natural disaster that could affect communities in Oregon. The recommendations are appropriately detailed for local consumption, the case studies are good, and the advice terse and to the point.

Palmer, Suzanne, and Pieter Severynen. 2001. *First National Congress on Fire Ecology, Prevention and Management.* Davis, Calif.: California Association for Fire Ecology.

Pima County, Arizona. 2003. *Ordinance No. 2003–70.* Tucson, Ariz.: Pima County.

Pima County, Arizona, Board of Directors. 2002. *Fire Management E.I.S. Issue Paper: Sonoran Desert Conservation Plan 2002.* Tucson, Ariz.: Pima County.

Pinetop-Lakeside, Arizona, City of. 2003. *Forest Health and Fire Protection.* Chapter 16.117.

Prescott, Arizona, City of. 2002. *Ordinance No. 4245.*

———. 2002. *Ordinance No. 4223.*

———. n.d. *Prescott Fire Department Vegetation Management Plan: Requirements for Compliance.*

Public Entity Risk Institute. 2001. *Reducing the Risk of Wildland-Urban Interface Fires.* Fairfax, Va.: Public Entity Risk Institute.

This is a collection of documents from an Internet symposium hosted by the Public Entity Risk Institute. Topics include wildfire suppression, Firewise concepts, mapping, and emergency management. One author points out the important role homeowners play in wildfire mitigation, viewing firefighting as a partnership between firefighters and the community at large. He also points out the problem of using FEMA or insurance funds to rebuild a larger home on the site where a home was destroyed. Another author states that, even though individual homeowners may want to reduce vegetation near their home to help protect it, they may be prevented from doing so by their homeowner's association. Another author states that both agencies and the public should focus on minimizing the impacts of fire, not eliminating fire altogether. The focus should be on managing the home ignition zone, which is the area within 100–200 feet of the home. The final author advocates for emergency management institutionally at all levels, from federal to local, so everyone is involved in a coordinated manner.

Pyne, Stephen J. 2004. Telephone interview with James Schwab, June 14.

———. 2004. *Tending Fire.* Washington, D.C.: Island Press.

———. 2001. *Fire: A Brief History.* Seattle: University of Washington Press.

Covering some of the same territory as *Fire in America*, Pyne here takes on a larger, more global, anthropological tour of the evolution of humankind's coexistence with fire. A good companion to the other book.

———. 1982. *Fire in America: A Cultural History of Wildland and Rural Fire.* Seattle: University of Washington Press.

This is undoubtedly the single best source of historical overview of the evolution of wildfires as an ecological influence in North America and of national fire policy in the U.S. Pyne takes us to the roots of both Native American and European American behavior with regard to fire, nature, and the forest; leads us through the intricacies of modern practices and experiences with wildfire; educates us on current firefighting practices; and leaves us on the doorstep of current developments in fire research and policy development.

Pyne, Stephen J., Patricia L. Andrew, and Richard D. Laven. 1996. *Introduction to Wildland Fire.* 2nd ed. New York: John Wiley & Sons.

Rancho Santa Fe Fire Protection District. 2002. *Ordinance No. 02–01.*

Rehm, Ronald G., Anthony Hamins, Howard R. Baum, Kevin B. McGrattan, and David D. Evans. 2002. "Community-Scale Fire Spread." NISTIR 6891. [Accessed December 1, 2004]. Available at http://fire.nist.gov/bfrlpubs/fire02/PDF/f02019.pdf.

Routt County Office of Emergency Management. 2003. *Routt County Fire Management Plan.* [Accessed December 2, 2004]. Available at www.co.routt.co.us/emergency/Plan-FMP2003.pdf. 2003.

Rural Fire Protection in America, Steering Committee. 1994. *Fire Protection in Rural America: A Challenge for the Future.* Washington, D.C.: National Association of State Foresters.

Sandoz, Mari. 1992. *Hostiles and Friendlies: Selected Short Writings of Mari Sandoz.* Lincoln: University of Nebraska Press.

Santa Barbara, City of. 2003. *Proposed Wildland Fire Plan.*

This is one of the best plans APA reviewed, extraordinary in its scope, detail, and practical orientation. The plan, intended to amend the city's general plan, ranks the city's existing high fire hazard areas based on hazard and risk, identifies policies and actions to reduce the city's threat from wildfire, and provides a process to better prioritize and fund implementation of wildland fire projects. What is extraordinary about this plan is the degree to which it breaks down the city into discrete areas where specific problems (i.e., those dealing with roof types, structure proximity, adequacy of water supply, fire response times, and fire ignitions) are identified along with corrective measures or mitigation. Excellent, easily readable maps show existing and proposed additional high fire hazard areas, areas in which vegetation needs management, and evaluation routes for the high hazard areas. A detailed program of vegetation management is set for all city parks or properties.

Schwab, Jim. 2002. "Summary of State Land-Use Planning Laws." [Accessed December 1, 2004]. Available at http://www.ibhs.org/publications/view.asp?id=302.

Schwab, Jim, with Lynn Ross and Lincoln Walther. 2003. *Firewise Post-Workshop Assessment Final Report*. Chicago: APA for Firewise Communities.

Schwab, Jim, with Kenneth C. Topping, Charles D. Eadie, Robert E. Deyle, and Richard A. Smith. 1998. *Planning for Post-Disaster Recovery and Reconstruction*. Planning Advisory Service Report No. 483/484. Chicago: American Planning Association.

Sellers, Stephen. 2004. Plenary #2: From the Ashes of the 2003 California Wildfires: Perspectives on the Future. Presentation at the 29th Annual Workshop on Hazards Research and Applications, Boulder, Colorado, July 13.

Simons, Tony. 2003. *Larimer County Fire Plan*. [Accessed November 23, 2004]. Available at www.larimer.org/wildfire/fire_plan.pdf.

This well-thought-out plan contains an extensive list of implementation measures with costs, responsible agencies, and a schedule. Several of the measures are notable. These include updating wildland fire hazard assessment maps and conducting subdivision fire assessments that would identify the most hazardous subdivisions and developments for targeted education.

Slack, Peter. 2000. *Firewise Construction: Design and Materials*. Denver: Colorado State Forest Service.

This publication provides homeowners and builders in the WUI with design and building techniques that can offer more protection from wildland or forest fires. The manual describes how to evaluate fire hazards, characterizes the elements of fire behavior, and assesses building site location factors affecting the intensity and duration of fires. A lengthy section of the manual explores building design and building materials and components.

Smith, Gary, and Tom Kuntz. 2002. *Wildland Fire Leadership Council Quarterly Meeting*. Fairfax, Va.: International Association of Fire Chiefs (IAFC).

This paper describes the role of the IAFC in the 10-Year Comprehensive Strategy. It also describes goals and actions that the IAFC recommends in conjunction with the 10-Year Comprehensive Plan.

Society of American Foresters. 2004. *Preparing a Community Wildfire Protection Plan: A Handbook for Wildland-Urban Interface Communities*. Bethesda, Md.: Society of American Foresters.

———. 2003. *Pilot Projects for Evaluating Innovative Federal Land Management Opportunities*. Bethesda, Md.: Society of American Foresters.

———. 2001. *National Fire Plan Implementation: Background for Transition*. Bethesda, Md.: Society of American Foresters.

Southeastern Land and Management. 2003. *Prowers County Colorado Pre-Disaster Mitigation Plan*. Prowers County, Colo.

Southern Group of State Foresters. n.d. *When the Forest Becomes a Community: A Forester's Handbook for the Wildland/Urban Interface*.

Basically, this is a guide for foresters dealing with the issues raised by development encroaching on wildland areas historically vulnerable to wildfires and how they affect forest management.

Spokane County Fire Prevention Committee. 1991. *Fire Protection in Land Planning and Building Construction*. Spokane, Wash.: Spokane County.

State of California. n.d. *California Fire Plan*. Sacramento: State Board of Forestry and California Department of Forestry and Fire Protection.

————. 2003. *Fire Hazard Planning: General Plan Technical Advice Series*. Sacramento: Governor's Office of Planning and Research.

This monograph provides guidance to cities and counties in California on how to incorporate fire hazard policies into the general or comprehensive plan required by state law. The monograph provides a list of general considerations for fire hazard and specific considerations for wildlands, urban interface areas, urban areas, post-event recovery and maintenance, fire effects and flood hazards, landslides, and terrorist risks. For each topical area, the monograph addresses required data and analyses and offers sample language that may be incorporated into general plan policies. Good treatment of interrelationships of fire hazards to various general plan elements.

State of California, The Resources Agency, and California Department of Forestry and Fire Protection. 1993. *Fire Safe Guides for Residential Development in California*. Sacramento: California Department of Forestry and Fire Protection.

Excellent monograph on the specifics of strategic fire management planning in California and on the West Coast in general. It describes the elements of such plans to include: (1) preparation, particularly involving local and state fire protection agencies and local governments; (2) definition of fire environment, including the development of maps that show fire histories and fire potential; (3) illustration of potential fire problems and correlation of fire potentials with various plan elements; (4) design of strategic fire measures (the manual recommends disregarding existing planning, zoning, and development practices); (5) identification of areas needing new fire facilities; and (6) compilation of proposals for changes in the local government's general or comprehensive plan.

State of Utah, Department of Natural Resources, Division of Forestry, Fire and State Lands. n.d. *Community Fire Planning for the Wildland-Urban Interface Guidance Document: Protecting Life, Property and Community Values Through Community-Based Planning*. Salt Lake City: State of Utah, Department of Natural Resources, Division of Forestry, Fire and State Lands.

Steelman, Toddi A., and Ginger Kunkel. 2003. *Project Summary: Community Responses to Wildland Fire Threats in New Mexico*. Raleigh: North Carolina State University.

This article is a compilation of "responsive practices" in Silver City, Ruidoso, Red River, and Santa Fe. Findings are summarized in text and tabular form. Each case study details what efforts are being made at wildfire preparedness and the unique aspects of each city. Red River, for example, is populated with mixed conifer and spruce fir, which are a traditionally "wet" fuel source, resistant to fire. Due to change in weather patterns, these trees have become more prone to wildfire and require thinning. Northeast of Santa Fe lies the Santa Fe watershed, which has become overpopulated with trees. The watershed provides approximately 40% of Santa Fe's water; therefore, a wildland fire there represents a threat to the city's water supply. A detailed description of partnerships, programs, and other issues within each city is provided.

Steelman, Toddi, and Devona Bell. 2003. *LaPlata County Trip Report, March 10–14, 2003, Colorado*.

This is a report of fire prevention efforts in LaPlata County, Colorado. Various programs are utilized by LaPlata County, including a fire plan that is regularly discussed by a local group to monitor implementation. Cities within the county have begun to review mitigation plans of developers who wish to build a new subdivision or individuals who want to build homes, but codes and standards are difficult to enforce due to lack of authority. Efforts have been made to help restore forests after wildfire. A mapping system is used to prioritize land areas in need of treatment to protect from wildfire threat. According to the authors, it will take the United States Forest Service 30–50 years to treat all fuels in the WUI in the San Juan National Forest.

Stewart, Susan I. 2004. E-mail communication with Jim Schwab, October 28.

Stewart, Susan I., Volker C. Radeloff, and Roger B. Hammer. 2003. "Characteristics and Location of the Wildland-Urban Interface in the United States." [Accessed December 1, 2004]. Available at http://silvis.forest.wisc.edu/Publications/PDFs/Stewart_etal_2003.pdf.

Summerfelt, Paul. 2001. *The Wildland/Urban Interface: What's Really at Risk.* Flagstaff, Ariz.: City of Flagstaff.

Teie, William C., and Brian F. Weatherford. 2000. *Fire in the West: The Wildland/Urban Interface Fire Problem.* A Report for the Council of Western State Foresters. Rescue, Calif.: Deer Valley Press.

U.S. Census Bureau. 2001. "Population Change and Distribution: Census 2000 Brief." Washington, D.C.: U.S. Census Bureau. April.

United States Department of Agriculture (USDA) Forest Service. 2003. *Homeowners, Communities, and Wildfire: Science Findings From the National Fire Plan.* St. Paul, Minn.: North Central Research Station, Forest Service, USDA.

A series of essay contributions from experts on public perceptions and practices with regard to the issue of defensible space, landscape values, prescribed burning, and similar topics. All papers are from a symposium held at Bloomington, Indiana, at Indiana University in June 2002.

———. 2000. *Managing the Impact of Wildfires on Communities and the Environment: A Report to the President in Response to the Wildfires of 2000.* Washington, D.C.: USDA Forest Service.

This document was created in response to the fires of the summer of 2000. It provides a history of wildfires in the United States and discusses the role weather has played in wildfires. As a result of the damages and losses suffered, the United States began extinguishing all wildfires as quickly as possible. In 1995, the Clinton administration reviewed current policies and created the Federal Wildland Fires Policy Statement, which included three main elements: (1) integration of firefighting management and preparedness, (2) reduction of hazardous fuel accumulation, and (3) coordination of and outreach to the local community. The National Wildfire Coordination Group was created to standardize training, equipment, and standards "to ensure that all Federal, State, and local agencies can easily operate together." The authors discuss the importance of reducing the risk of wildfire through managing the amount of fuel available. They advocate prescribed burn as a necessary means of reducing hazardous fuels, preventing fire, and maintaining forest health. The importance of developing local firefighting brigades and creating individual property owner responsibility is discussed.

The second half of the report describes the consequences experienced in the 2000 wildfire season, such as economic losses (to the tourism industry in particular) and damage to natural resources, including increased risk of flood and mudslides due to lack of hillside vegetation. Finally, the report makes recommendations for future wildfire seasons. Among the recommendations are continued allocation of resources to firefighting efforts, stabilization and restoration of the burned area, and prevention, which would include creating a market for small diameter trees removed from the forest to decrease the amount of hazardous fuels present.

U.S. Department of Agriculture (USDA) Forest Service and U.S. Department of the Interior (DOI), Bureau of Land Management. 2004. *The Healthy Forests Initiative and Healthy Forests Restoration Act: Interim Field Guide.* Washington, D.C.: USDA.

United States General Accounting Office. 1999. *Federal Wildfire Activities: Current Strategy and Issues Needing Attention.* Washington, D.C.: United States General Accounting Office.

University of California. 2000. *Fire Hazard Zoning Field Guide.* Berkeley: Forest Products Laboratory.

This guide describes the practice of fire hazard zoning in California, both in areas where the state has responsibility and where local government has responsibility. According to the guide, fire hazard zoning is a planning and regulatory activity conducted by a local government that provides criteria for the regulation of development or other activities in areas of various hazard classifications. The guide discuses how and why state mandated fire hazard zoning and mitigation strategies have been enacted. It also describes various fire hazard assessment and classification systems that can be used.

———. 2000. *Structural Fire Prevention Field Guide for Mitigation of Wildland Fires.* Sacramento: California Department of Forestry and Fire Protection.

This document is part of a larger series of California state publications, largely coordinated through the state fire marshal's office, which incorporate land-use planning into the overall analysis of wildland fire policy. California requires a safety element in local land-use plans, but this guide also discusses the incorporation of fire-safe planning into other local master plan elements in a very thorough way that puts California at the forefront of wildfire planning literature. Particularly useful for local planners is a series of essential questions to be answered in developing each of several plan elements that should take wildfire into account.

University of California, and Interagency Engineering Working Group. 2000. *Property Inspection Guide.* [Accessed December 2, 2004]. Available at http://osfm.fire.ca.gov/property.html.

University of Florida. 2001. *Wildfire in Florida: Issues of Law and Forestry Practices.* Gainesville: University of Florida Conservation Clinic.

This is a good treatment of legal dimensions of forestry practices, particularly the authority of the state of Florida and local governments to conduct prescribed burning in areas that might be subject to wildfire hazards. It identifies several local ordinances requiring, under certain conditions, prescribed burning. Legal analysis finds there is no common-law liability for failure to conduct prescribed burning. It describes a proposed Alachua County plan whose conservation and open space element contains an objective and several policies for wildfire mitigation.

Vasievich, Mike. 1999. "Here Comes the Neighborhood! A New Gold Rush and Eleven Other Trends Affecting the Midwest." *NC News* (North Central Forest Experiment Station), August/September, 1–3.

Virginia Department of Forestry. n.d. *Woodland Home Forest Fire Protection Planning Guide.* Richmond: Virginia Department of Forestry.

Virginia Firewise Landscaping Task Force. 1998. *Virginia Firescapes Firewise Landscaping for Woodland Homes.* Blacksburg: Virginia Cooperative Extension.

Vogt, Christine. 2002. "Seasonal and Permanent Home Owners' Past Experiences and Approval of Fuels Reduction." In *Homeowners, Communities, and Wildfire: Science Findings from the National Fire Plan,* compiled by Pamela J. Jakes. St. Paul, Minn.: USDA Forest Service, North Central Research Station.

Vogt, Christine, Greg Winter, and Jeremy Fried. 2002. "Antecedents to Attitudes Toward Prescribed Burning, Mechanical Thinning, and Defensible Space Fuel Reduction Techniques." In *Homeowners, Communities, and Wildfire: Science Findings from the National Fire Plan,* compiled by Pamela J. Jakes. St. Paul, Minn.: USDA Forest Service, North Central Research Station.

Washington State Department of Community, Trade and Economic Development. 1999. *Optional Comprehensive Plan Element for Natural Hazard Reduction.* Olympia: State of Washington. June.

Watson, George, and Guy McCarthy. 2004. "Taking a Gamble and Living Among Nature," *San Bernardino Sun*, June 27.

Wellington Wildfire Mitigation Technical Advisory Committee. 2003. *Village of Wellington Wildfire Mitigation Plan*. Wellington, Fla.: Village of Wellington.

The introductory portion of the plan lists the various groups involved in the creation of the plan who are critical to the structure of wildfire mitigation and who provide a direct link to local property owners. The next portion discusses various rating systems available to assess wildfire risks and explains why Wellington chose to use a combination of two—the Wildfire Hazard and Mitigation System (WHIMS) and the Florida Department of Forestry (DOF) system. WHIMS allows for parcel level analysis using GIS and the Florida DOF system allows for subdivision level analysis.

The document concludes with a chart that details potential mitigation options to address each problem or concern identified in previous phases. For each problem or concern there is at least one mitigation option with a vague implementation framework (lead responsibility, support, date, and method), and advantages and disadvantages associated with it (cost, feasibility, public acceptance, and environmental consequences.) The last few pages provide suggestions for an implementation program, including administrative framework, plan monitoring, funding, and a plan update process.

Wetmore, French. 1996. *Reducing Flood Losses Through Multi-Objective Management*. Madison, Wis.: Association of State Floodplain Managers.

Whelan, Robert J. 1995. *The Ecology of Fire*. Cambridge: Cambridge University Press.

The natural assumption for most people is to think of fire as a destructive force, yet it is also clearly a force of nature. The cover image on this book of the phoenix rising from the ashes suggests that ancient Greek mythology was on to something. What does fire contribute to nature? This book explores the ways in which plants develop or inherit tolerance to fire, fire's place in evolutionary biology, and fire's impact on wildlife populations. For those who want an accurate understanding of the natural properties and impacts of fire, this is a great starting point.

Wilderness Society, The. 2003. "Summary of the Hayman Fire, Colorado." [Accessed October 26, 2004]. Available at http:www.wilderness.org/Library/Documents/WildfireSummary_Hayman.cfm.

Yakima County, Washington. 2001. *Urban-Wildland Interface Code*. Yakima County Ordinance [4–2001].

Yoder, Jonathan, Marcia Tilley, David Engle, and Samuel Fuhlendorf. 2003. "Economics and Prescribed Fire Law in the United States." *Review of Agricultural Economics* 25, no. 1: 218–33.

Fire Danger Rating System

This appendix is an excerpt from the National Fire Danger Rating (NFDR) System, 1978, United States Department of Agriculture Forest Service, general technical report INT-39, and is for informational purposes and is not intended for adoption.

The fuel models that follow are only general descriptions because they represent all wildfire fuels from Florida to Alaska and from the East Coast to California.

FUEL MODEL KEY

I. Mosses, lichens, and low shrubs predominate ground fuels.

    A. An overstory of conifers occupies more than one-third of the site: MODEL Q

    B. There is no overstory, or it occupies less than one-third of the site (tundra): MODEL S

II. Marsh grasses and/or reeds predominate: MODEL N

III. Grasses and/or forbs predominate.

    A. There is an open overstory of conifer and/or hardwood trees: MODEL C

    B. There is no overstory.

        1. Woody shrubs occupy more than one-third but less than two-thirds of the site: MODEL T

        2. Woody shrubs occupy less than one-third of the site.

            a. The grasses and forbs are primarily annuals: MODEL A

            b. The grasses and forbs are primarily perennials: MODEL L

IV. Brush, shrubs, tree reproduction, or dwarf tree species predominate.

    A. Average height of woody plants is 6 feet or greater.

        1. Woody plants occupy two-thirds or more of the site.

            a. One-fourth or more of the woody foliage is dead.

                (1) Mixed California chaparral: MODEL B

                (2) Other types of brush: MODEL F

            b. Up to one-fourth of the woody foliage is dead: MODEL Q

            c. Little dead foliage: MODEL O

        2. Woody plants occupy less than two-thirds of the site: MODEL F

    B. Average height of woody plants is less than 6 feet.

        1. Woody plants occupy two-thirds or more of the site.

            a. Western United States: MODEL F

            b. Eastern United States: MODEL O

        2. Woody plants occupy less than two-thirds but more than one-third of the site.

            a. Western United States: MODEL T

            b. Eastern United States: MODEL D

        3. Woody plants occupy less than one-third of the site.

            a. The grasses and forbs are primarily annuals: MODEL A

            b. The grasses and forbs are primarily perennials: MODEL L

V. Trees predominate.

    A. Deciduous broadleaf species predominate.

        1. The area has been thinned or partially cut, leaving slash as the major fuel component: MODEL K

2. The area has not been thinned or partially cut.

    a. The overstory is dormant; the leaves have fallen: MODEL E

B. Conifer species predominate.

    1. Lichens, mosses, and low shrubs dominate as understory fuels: MODEL Q

    2. Grasses and forbs are the primary ground fuels: MODEL C

    3. Woody shrubs and/or reproduction dominate as understory fuels.

        a. The understory burns readily.

            (1) Western United States: MODEL T

            (2) Eastern United States:

                (a) The understory is more than 6 feet tall: MODEL O

                (b) The understory is less than 6 feet tall: MODEL D

        b. The understory seldom burns: MODEL H

    4. Duff and litter, branchwood, and tree boles are the primary ground fuels.

        a. The overstory is overmature and decadent; there is a heavy accumulation of dead tree debris: MODEL G

        b. The overstory is not decadent; there is only a nominal accumulation of debris.

            (1) The needless are 2 inches (51 mm) or more in length (most pines).

                (a) Eastern United States: MODEL P

                (b) Western United States: MODEL U

            (2) The needles are less than 2 inches (51 mm) long: MODEL H

VI. Slash is the predominant fuel.

    A. The foliage is still attached; there has been little settling.

        1. The loading is 25 tons/acre (56.1 tons/ha) or greater: MODEL I

        2. The loading is less than 25 tons/acre (56.1 tons/ha) but more than 15 tons/acre (33.7 tons/ha): MODEL J

        3. The loading is less than 15 tons/acre (33.7 tons/ha): MODEL K

    B. Settling is evident; the foliage is falling off; grasses, forbs, and shrubs are invading the area.

        1. The loading is 25 tons/acre (56.1 tons/ha) or greater: MODEL J

        2. The loading is less than 25 tons/acre (56.1 tons/ha): MODEL K

FUEL MODEL A

This fuel model represents western grasslands vegetated by annual grasses and forbs. Brush or trees may be present but are very sparse, occupying less than a third of the area. Examples of types where Fuel Model A should be used are cheatgrass and medusahead. Open pinyon-juniper, sagebrush-grass, and desert shrub associations may appropriately be assigned this fuel model if the woody plants meet the density criteria. The quantity and continuity of the ground fuels vary greatly with rainfall from year to year.

FUEL MODEL B

Mature, dense fields of brush 6 feet (1829 mm) or more in height are represented by this fuel model. One-fourth or more of the aerial fuel in such stands is dead. Foliage burns readily. Model B fuels are potentially very dangerous, fostering intense, fast-spreading fires. This model is for California mixed chaparral generally 30 years or older. The F model is more appropriate for pure chamise stands. The B model may also be used for the New Jersey pine barrens.

FUEL MODEL C

Open pine stands typify Model C fuels. Perennial grasses and forbs are the primary ground fuel, but there is enough needle litter and branchwood present to contribute significantly to the fuel loading. Some brush and shrubs may be present, but they are of little consequence. Situations covered by Fuel Model C are open, longleaf, slash, ponderosa, Jeffrey, and sugar pine stands. Some pinyon-juniper stands may qualify.

FUEL MODEL D

This fuel model is specifically for the palmetto-gallberry understory-pine overstory association of the southeast coastal plains. It can also be used for the so-called "low pocosins" where Fuel Model O might be too severe. This model should only be used in the Southeast, because of a high moisture of extinction.

FUEL MODEL E

Use this model after leaf fall for hardwood and mixed hardwood-conifer types where the hardwoods dominate. The fuel is primarily hardwood leaf litter. The oat-hickory types are best represented by Fuel Model E, but E is an acceptable choice for northern hardwoods and mixed forests of the Southeast. In high winds, the fire danger may be underrated because rolling and blowing leaves are not accounted for. In the summer after the trees have leafed out, Fuel Model E should be replaced by Fuel Model R.

FUEL MODEL F

Fuel Model F is the only one of the 1972 NFDR System Fuel Models whose application has changed. Model F now represents mature closed chamise stands and oakbrush fields of Arizona, Utah, and Colorado. It also applies to young, closed stands and mature, open stands of California mixed chaparral. Open stands of pinyon-juniper are represented; however, fire activity will be overrated at low wind speeds and where there is sparse ground fuel.

FUEL MODEL G

Fuel Model G is used for dense conifer stands where there is a heavy accumulation of litter and downed woody material. Such stands are typically overmature and may also be suffering insect, disease, wind or ice damage—natural events that create a very heavy buildup of dead material on the forest floor. The duff and litter are deep, and much of the woody material is more than 3 inches (76 mm) in diameter. The undergrowth is variable, but shrubs are usually restricted to openings. Types meant to be represented by Fuel Model G are hemlock-Sitka spruce, Coast Douglas-fir, and wind-thrown or bug-killed stands of lodgepole pine and spruce.

FUEL MODEL H

The short-needled conifers (white pines, spruces, larches, and firs) are represented by Fuel Model H. In contrast to Model G fuels, Fuel Model H describes a healthy stand with sparse undergrowth and a thin layer of ground fuels. Fires in H fuels are typically slow spreading and are dangerous only in scattered areas where the downed woody material is concentrated.

FUEL MODEL I

Fuel Model I was designed for clear-cut conifer slash where the total loading of materials less than 6 inches (152 mm) in diameter exceeds 25 tons/acre (56.1 metric tons/ha). After settling and the fines (needles and twigs) fall from the branches, Fuel Model I will overrate the fire potential. For lighter loadings of clear-cut conifer slash, use Fuel Model J, and for light thinnings and partial cuts where the slash is scattered under a residual overstory, use Fuel Model K.

FUEL MODEL J

This model is complementary to Fuel Model I. It is for clear-cuts and heavily thinned conifer stands where the total loading of materials less than 6 inches (152 mm) in diameter is less than 25 tons/acre (56.1 metric tons/ha). Again, as the slash ages, the fire potential will be overrated.

FUEL MODEL K

Slash fuels from light thinnings and partial cuts in conifer stands are represented by Fuel Model K. Typically, the slash is scattered about under an open overstory. This model applies to hardwood slash and to southern pine clear-cuts where the loading of all fuels is less than 15 tons/acre (33.7 tons/ha).

FUEL MODEL L

This fuel model is meant to represent western grasslands vegetated by perennial grasses. The principal species are coarser and the loadings heavier than those in Model A fuels.

Otherwise, the situations are very similar; shrubs and trees occupy less than one-third of the area. The quantity of fuel in these areas is more stable from year to year. In sagebrush areas, Fuel Model T may be more appropriate.

FUEL MODEL N
This fuel model was constructed specifically for the saw-grass prairies of south Florida. It may be useful in other marsh situations where the fuel is coarse and reedlike. This model assumes that one-third of the aerial portion of the plants is dead. Fast-spreading, intense fires can occur even over standing water.

FUEL MODEL O
The O fuel model applies to dense, brushlike fuels of the Southeast. O fuels, except for a deep litter layer, are almost entirely living, in contrast to B fuels. The foliage burns readily, except during the active growing season. The plants are typically over 6 feet (1829 mm) tall and are often found under an open stand of pine. The high pocosins of the Virginia, North and South Carolina coasts are the ideal of Fuel Model O. If the plants do not meet the 6-foot (1829 mm) criterion in those areas, Fuel Model D should be used.

FUEL MODEL P
Closed, thrifty stands of long-needled southern pines are characteristic of P fuels. A 2- to 4-inch (51 to 102 mm) layer of lightly compacted needle litter is the primary fuel. Some small-diameter branchwood is present, but the density of the canopy precludes more than a scattering of shrubs and grass. Fuel Model P has the high moisture of extinction characteristic of the Southeast. The corresponding model for other long-needled pines is U.

FUEL MODEL Q
Upland Alaskan black spruce is represented by Fuel Model Q. The stands are dense but have frequent openings filled with usually flammable shrub species. The forest floor is a deep layer of moss and lichens, but there is some needle litter and small-diameter branchwood. The branches are persistent on the trees, and ground fires easily reach into the tree crowns. This fuel model may be useful for jack pine stands in the Lake States. Ground fires are typically slow spreading, but a dangerous crowning potential exists.

FUEL MODEL R
This fuel model represents the hardwood areas after the canopies leaf out in the spring. It is provided as the off-season substitute for E. It should be used during the summer in all hardwood and mixed conifer-hardwood stands where more than half of the overstory is deciduous.

FUEL MODEL S
Alaskan or alpine tundra on relatively well-drained sites is the S fuel. Grass and low shrubs are often present, but the principal fuel is a deep layer of lichens and moss. Fires in these fuels are not fast spreading or intense, but are difficult to extinguish.

FUEL MODEL T
The bothersome sagebrush-grass types of the Great Basin and the Intermountain West are characteristic of T fuels. The shrubs burn easily and are not dense enough to shade out grass and other herbaceous plants. The shrubs must occupy at least one-third of the site or the A or L fuel models should be used. Fuel Model T might be used for immature scrub oak and desert shrub associations in the West, and the scrub oak-wire grass type in the Southeast.

FUEL MODEL U
Closed stands of western long-needled pines are covered by this model. The ground fuels are primarily litter and small branchwood. Grass and shrubs are precluded by the dense canopy but occur in the occasional natural opening. Fuel Model U should be used for ponderosa, Jeffrey, sugar pine, and red pine stands of the Lake States. Fuel Model P is the corresponding model for southern pine plantations.

Fire Hazard Severity Form

A. Subdivision Design   **Points**

1. Ingress/Egress
  Two or more primary roads   ——— 1
  One road   ——— 3
  One-way road in, one-way road out ——— 5

2. Width of Primary Road
  20 feet or more   ——— 1
  Less than 20 feet   ——— 3

3. Accessibility
  Road grade 5% or less   ——— 1
  Road grade more than 5%   ——— 3

4. Secondary Road Terminus
  Loop roads, cul-de-sacs with an outside turning radius
    of 45 feet or more   ——— 1
  Cul-de-sac turnaround
  Dead-end roads 200 feet or less in length ——— 3
  Dead-end roads more than 200 feet in length ——— 5

5. Street Signs
  Present   ——— 1
  Not present   ——— 3

B. Vegetation (IUWIC Definitions)

1. Fuel Types
  Light   ——— 1
  Medium   ——— 5
  Heavy   ———10

2. Defensible Space
  70% or more of site   ——— 1
  30% or more, but less than 70% of site ———10
  Less than 30% of site   ———20

C. Topography [It seems like something is missing from here.]

  8% or less   ——— 1
  More than 8%, but less than 20% ——— 4
  20% or more, but less than 30% ——— 7
  30% or more   ———10

D. Roofing Material

  Class A Fire Rated   ——— 1
  Class B Fire Rated   ——— 5
  Class C Fire Rated   ———10
  Nonrated   ———20

E. Fire Protection - Water Source

  500 GPM hydrant within 1,000 feet ——— 1
  Hydrant farther than 1,000 feet of draft site ——— 2
  Water source 20 min. or less, round trip ——— 5
  Water source more than 20 min., but 45 min. or less,
    round trip   ——— 7
  Water source more than 45 min., round trip ———10

F. Existing Building Construction Materials

Noncombustible siding/deck	—— 1
Noncombustible siding/combustible deck	—— 5
Combustible siding and deck	——10

G. Utilities (gas and/or electric)

All underground utilities	—— 1
One underground, one aboveground	—— 3
All aboveground	—— 5

Total for Subdivision   ——

Moderate Hazard	40–59
High Hazard	60–74
Extreme Hazard	75+

Source: International Code Council (ICC), *International Urban-Wildland Interface Code* (Country Club Hills, IL: ICC, 2003), Appendix C.

American Planning Association Growing Smart^{SM} Model Statute for a Natural Hazards Element of a Comprehensive Plan

Commentary

Planning for the reduction of losses from natural hazards has been largely driven by concerns for public safety. California, for example, uses the term "safety element" to describe a required local comprehensive plan element that involves the assessment of a variety of natural hazards.[225] Other issues that justify such planning—including fiscal and economic instability—are derived mostly from the consequences of failing to adequately exercise the police power to ensure public safety in the face of natural disasters. This remains true even with planning for long-term recovery and post-disaster reconstruction: the aftermath of one natural disaster is simply the prelude to the next one.

States and communities across the country are slowly, but increasingly, realizing that simply responding to natural disasters, without addressing ways to minimize their potential effect, is no longer an adequate role for government. Striving to prevent unnecessary damage from natural disasters through proactive planning that characterizes the hazard, assesses the community's vulnerability, and designs appropriate land-use policies and building code requirements is a more effective and fiscally sound approach to achieving public safety goals related to natural hazards.[226] Attending to natural hazard mitigation can also provide benefits in other local policy areas. Minimizing or eliminating development in floodplain corridors, for example, provides environmental benefits as well as potential new recreational opportunities. Communities can often profit from undertaking post-disaster reconstruction actions that at other times might be too controversial or cumbersome—the notion of striking while the iron is hot. Where a disaster has destroyed a marginal business district, for example, planners can seize the opportunity to use redevelopment to effect a rebirth that might not otherwise be possible.

Building public consensus behind even the most solid plans can be a challenging task, especially in jurisdictions exposed to multiple hazards. To meet this challenge, it is recommended that the development of a natural hazards element, including plans for post-disaster recovery and reconstruction, come from an interdisciplinary, interagency team with broadly based citizen participation, to ensure both a range of input and effective public support. Community experience in dealing with natural hazards plans, whether for mitigation or post-disaster recovery, or both, has consistently demonstrated that this topic demands a wide range of input and expertise.

---

[225]Calif. Govt. Code Section 65302 (g) requires a safety element "for the protection of the community from any unreasonable risks associated with the effects of seismically induced surface rupture, ground shaking, ground failure, tsunami, seiche, and dam failure; slope instability leading to mudslides and landslides; subsidence, liquefaction and other seismic hazards identified pursuant to Chapter 7.8 (commencing with Section 2690) of the Public Resources Code, and other geologic hazards known to the legislative body; flooding; and wild land and urban fires." In addition to the mapping of seismic and geologic hazards, the element is to address "evacuation routes, peakload water supply requirements, and minimum road widths and clearances around structures, as those items relate to identified fire and geologic hazards."

[226]See generally Roger A. Nazwadzky, "Lawyering Your Municipality Through a Natural Disaster or Emergency," *Urban Lawyer* 27, No. 1 (Winter 1995): 9–27.

The following model incorporates the best practices found in state statutes[227] plus other best practices drawn from exemplary local planning for natural hazards and long-term post-disaster recovery. These latter best practices are identified in the commentary to the model natural hazards element below.

7–210 Natural Hazards Element [Opt-Out Provision Applies]

(1) A natural hazards element shall be included in the local comprehensive plan, except as provided in Section [7–202(5)] above.

(2) The purposes of the natural hazards element are to:

(a) document the physical characteristics, magnitude, severity, frequency, causative factors, and geographic extent of all natural hazards, from whatever cause, within or potentially affecting the community, including, but not limited to, flooding, [seismicity, wildfires, wind-related hazards such as tornadoes, coastal storms, winter storms, and hurricanes, and landslides or subsidence resulting from the instability of geological features];

● Obviously, the presence and prevalence of specific natural hazards varies widely not only among states, but even within states at both regional and local levels. This section lists all major categories while allowing states to use only those that apply, although it is clearly better to list in the statute any hazards that may apply *somewhere* in the state. Flooding, however, is a universally applicable concern. It should be noted that "natural" hazards include hazards caused or exacerbated by human action, such as forest fires sparked by campfires and ground subsidence caused by old mines.

(b) identify those elements of the built and natural environment and, as a result, human lives, that are at risk from the identified natural hazards, as well as the extent of existing and future vulnerability that may result from current zoning and development policies;

(c) determine the adequacy of existing transportation facilities and public buildings to accommodate disaster response and early recovery needs such as evacuation and emergency shelter;

(d) develop technically feasible and cost-effective measures for mitigation of the identified hazards based on the public determination of the level of acceptable risk;

(e) identify approaches and tools for post-disaster recovery and reconstruction that incorporate future risk reduction; and

(f) identify the resources needed for effective ongoing hazard mitigation and for implementing the plan for post-disaster recovery and reconstruction.

(3) The natural hazards element shall be in both map and textual form. Maps shall be at a suitable scale consistent with the existing land-use map or map series described in Section 7–204 (6)(a) above.

(4) In preparing the natural hazards element, the local planning agency shall undertake supporting studies that are relevant to the topical areas included in the element. In undertaking these studies, the local planning agency may

---

[227]The following state statutes provide for natural hazards planning: Arizona (Ariz.Rev.Stat. Section 11–806B), California (Cal.Gov't.Code Section 65302(e)(7) & (g)), Colorado (Colo.Rev. Stat. Section Section 30–28–106, 31–23–206), Florida (Fla.Stat.Ann. Section Section 163.3177(6)(g), 7(h), 163.3178), Georgia (Ga. Code Ann. Section 12–2–8), Idaho (Idaho Code Section 67–6508(g)), Indiana (Ind.Code Section 36–7–4–503), Iowa (Iowa Code Section 281.4), Kentucky (Ky.Rev.Stat.Ann. Section 100.187(5)), Louisiana (La.Rev.Stat.Ann. Section 33:107), Maine (Me.Rev.Stat.Ann. tit. 30A Section 4326A(1)(d)), Maryland (Md. Code Ann. tit. 66B Section 3.05(a)(1)(viii)), Michigan (Mich.Comp.Laws Section 125.36), Montana (Mont. Code Ann. Section 76–1–601(2)(h)), Nevada (Nev.Rev.Stat. Section 278.160.1 (k) & (l)), North Carolina (N.C.Gen.Stat. Section 113A–110ff), Oregon (Or.Rev.Stat. Section 197.175), Pennsylvania (53 Pa.Stat.Ann. Section 10301(2)), Rhode Island (R.I.Gen.Laws Section 45–22.2–6(E)), South Carolina (S.C. Code Ann. Section 6–7–510), Utah (Utah Code Ann. Section 10–9–302(2)(c)), Vermont (Vt.Stat.Ann. tit. 24, Section 4382(a)(2)), Virginia (Va. Code Ann. Section 15.1–446.1.1), Washington (Wash.Rev. Code Section 36.70.330(1)), West Virginia (W.Va. Code Section 8–24–17(a)(9)).

use studies conducted by others. The supporting studies may concern, but shall not be limited to, the following:

    (a) maps of all natural hazard areas, accompanied by an account of past disaster events, including descriptions of the events, damage estimates, probabilities of occurrence, causes of damage, and subsequent rebuilding efforts;

● With regard to flooding and coastal storm surge zones, the local jurisdiction may simply incorporate the existing National Flood Insurance Program (NFIP) maps and U.S. Army Corps of Engineers/National Weather Service storm surge maps. State and U.S. Geological Survey maps should provide at least a starting point for areas with seismic hazards. Portland Metro, in cooperation with the Oregon Department of Geology and Mineral Industries (DOGAMI), has undertaken an effort funded by Federal Emergency Management Agency (FEMA) to complete seismic hazard mapping of the entire Portland region using geographic information systems (GIS).[228] The department is also mapping tsunami hazard areas along the Oregon coast as a FEMA-funded sequel to the first such project, completed in early 1995 in Eureka, California.[229] In states with volcanoes, the mapping should include lava, pyroclastic, and debris flows and projected patterns of ash fallout in the surrounding region, including the potential for flooding from the blockage of rivers. Other sources for potential problems include the National Weather Service for storm and wind patterns and some innovative new GIS techniques in Colorado for mapping wildfire hazards.[230]

    (b) an assessment of those elements of the built and natural environments (including buildings and infrastructure) that are at risk within the natural hazard areas identified in subparagraph (a) above as well as the extent of future vulnerability that may result from current land development regulations and practices within the local government's jurisdiction;

● The study in subparagraph (4)(b) is also known among disaster officials and experts as a "vulnerability assessment" and serves two purposes: (1) to identify vulnerable structures and; (2) to determine the cause and extent of their vulnerability. For example, the California Governor's Office of Emergency Services has outlined procedures used by various communities for inventorying seismic hazards.[231] The subparagraph emphasizes the importance of including the impact of natural hazards in a buildout analysis in order to assess the potential consequences of current laws and policies, including those pertaining to the extension of public infrastructure in hazard-prone areas.

This requirement can be tailored to the actual hazards a state may be dealing with, as California and Nevada have done with seismic safety. One striking example is a 1979 Los Angeles ordinance that mandated both an inventory and a retrofitting program that over time has upgraded the seismic stability of the city's housing stock. The format for this with regard to flood hazard areas is already reasonably clear as a result of NFIP regulations, which include requirements for elevating substantially damaged or improved buildings above the base flood elevation.

---

[228]See *Using Earthquake Hazard Maps for Land Use Planning and Building Permit Administration*, Report of the Metro Advisory Committee for Mitigating Earthquake Damage (Portland, Ore.: Portland Metro, May 1996) and *Metro Area Disaster Geographic Information System*: Volume One (Portland, Ore.: Portland Metro, June 1996).

[229]National Oceanic and Atmospheric Administration (NOAA), Pacific Marine Environmental Laboratory. *Tsunami Hazard Mitigation: A Report to the Senate Appropriations Committee* (Seattle, Wash.: NOAA, The Laboratory, March 31, 1995).

[230]Colorado has been increasing its attention to both the wildfire issue and hazards generally. See *Land Use Guidelines for Natural and Technological Hazards Planning* (Denver: Colorado Department of Local Affairs, Office of Emergency Management, March 1994). An interesting source on the mapping of wildfire hazards is Boulder County's World Wide Web site at http:boco.co.gov/gislu/whims.html. [This is a dead link. Not sure how to format this since the entire appendix is an excerpt, but the new site appears to be www.co.boulder.co.us/lu/wildfire/whims.htm.]

[231]*Earthquake Recovery: A Survival Manual for Local Government* (Sacramento: California Governor's Office of Emergency Services, September 1993), Chs. 9–10.

Analysis of wind-related problems is more likely to result in building code changes to strengthen wind resistance, as in southern Florida.

    (c) state or other local mitigation strategies which identify activities to reduce the effects of natural hazards;

    (d) an inventory of emergency public shelters, an assessment of their functional and locational adequacy, and an identification of the remedial action needed to overcome any deficiencies in the functions and locations of the shelters;

    (e) an identification of all evacuation routes and systems for the populations of hazard-prone areas that might reasonably be expected to be evacuated in the event of an emergency and an analysis of their traffic capacity and accessibility;

- This study is a good place to marry the expertise of planners (including transportation planners) and emergency managers. While the latter can identify the resources and the needs in this area, the former can help integrate that knowledge into routine planning for hazard-prone areas. Lee County, Florida, has used such studies to evaluate its shelter availability for disaster purposes. Because of limited access to its offshore location, Sanibel, Florida, has gone even further in using evacuation and shelter capacity as the basis for growth caps.

An interesting example of a natural hazards element component dealing with these issues appears in Florida Stats. §163.3178 (2)(d), which requires a "component which outlines principles for hazard mitigation and protection of human life against the effects of natural disaster, including population evacuation, which take into consideration the capability to safely evacuate the density of coastal population proposed in the future land use plan element in the event of an impending natural disaster."

    (f) analyses of the location of special populations that need assistance in evacuation and in obtaining shelter;

    (g) an inventory of the technical, administrative, legal, and financial resources available or potentially available to assist both ongoing mitigation efforts as well as post-disaster recovery and reconstruction;[232] and

- Jurisdictions across the country have experimented with a number of means of facilitating and empowering efforts to reduce their vulnerability to natural hazards. Some of these involve the use of performance and design standards that give planners and planning commissions greater authority to insist that new development meet strict standards of hazard mitigation. For example, Wake County, North Carolina, requires that, in drainage areas of 100 acres or more, the applicant must show that any rise in water level resulting from building on the property can be contained on that property, with the applicant's only alternative being to secure easements from neighboring property owners to allow for that rise. Portola Valley, California, is a good example of seismic and hillside hazard mitigation in its use of cluster zoning for new subdivisions in certain areas.[233] Jurisdictions also have experimented with means of financing such efforts. A clear starting point is to center somewhere in local government a periodically updated repository of information about outside funding sources both from government and the private sector, including voluntary resources from nonprofit organizations. The advantage is that the community can then, in the event of a disaster, tap these resources expeditiously, preferably with the added advantage of an already developed plan for reconstruction. In addition, this study will serve to highlight funding mechanisms through local government, such as the All Hazards Protection

---

[232]For a discussion of approaches to drafting floodplain management ordinances, see Jim Schwab, "Zoning for Flood Hazards," *Zoning News* (Chicago: American Planning Association, October 1997). See also Marya Morris, *Subdivision Design in Flood Hazard Areas*, Planning Advisory Service Report No. 473 (Chicago: American Planning Association, September 1997).

[233]William Spangle and Associates, Inc., *Geology and Planning: The Portola Valley Experience* (Portola Valley, Cal.: William Spangle and Associates, 1988).

District and Fund created by Lee County, Florida, in 1990 to support local hazard mitigation programs.[234] That fund depends on a property tax levy; in 1993, Lee County also considered, but did not pass, a proposal for an impact fee targeted at hazard-prone areas to fund emergency public shelters.

> (h) a study of the most feasible and effective alternatives for organizing, in advance of potential natural disasters, the management of the process of post-disaster long-term recovery and reconstruction.

● Numerous studies have examined at some length the potentials and pitfalls of various structural arrangements for organizing interagency, interdisciplinary task forces to oversee the process of long-term recovery and reconstruction following a disaster. A forthcoming (1998) APA Planning Advisory Service Report, *Planning for Post-Disaster Recovery and Reconstruction*, sponsored by the Federal Emergency Management Agency, deals with this issue and provides an extensive bibliography. Such plans have also been developed in Los Angeles[235]; Nags Head, North Carolina; and Hilton Head Island, South Carolina, among other jurisdictions, and are mandated for coastal communities in Florida and North Carolina. Two overriding principles seem to emerge from such efforts to date: (1) that successful implementation depends heavily on support from top local officials, whether that be the mayor or city manager; and (2) that a recovery task force should include representatives of all major agencies potentially involved in the reconstruction effort, specifically including but not limited to safety and emergency management forces, planning, building inspectors, public works, and transportation. It is vitally important in the aftermath of a disaster that all these agencies know not only what the others are doing, but who should report to whom for what purposes.

(5) The natural hazards element shall consist of:

> (a) a statement, with supporting analysis, of the goals, policies, and guidelines of the local government to address natural hazards and to take action to mitigate their effects. The statement shall describe the physical characteristics, magnitude, severity, probability, frequency, causative factors, and geographic extent of all natural hazards affecting the local government as well as the elements of the built and natural environment within the local government's jurisdiction that are at risk;

> (b) a determination of linkages between any natural hazards areas identified pursuant to subparagraph (a) above and any other elements of the local comprehensive plan;

> (c) a determination of any conflicts between any natural hazards areas and any future land-use pattern or public improvement or capital project proposed in any element of the local comprehensive plan;

> (d) priorities of actions for eliminating or minimizing inappropriate and unsafe development in identified natural hazard zones when opportunities arise, including the identification and prioritization of properties deemed appropriate for acquisition, or structures and buildings deemed suitable for elevation, retrofitting, or relocation;

● This language is drawn from Florida Stats. §163.3178 (2), which outlines the components of the coastal management element required of all communities within coastal counties, and (8). Subdivision (2)(f) states that a redevelopment component "shall be used to eliminate inappropriate and unsafe development in the *coastal* areas when opportunities arise" (emphasis added). Paragraph (8) requires that each

---

[234]Lee County, Fla., Resolution No. 90–12–19.

[235]The Northridge earthquake in February 1994, which occurred shortly after the adoption of the Los Angeles plan, afforded the rare opportunity for the National Science Foundation to underwrite two independent analyses of the plan's utility and effectiveness in the aftermath of that disaster. Spangle Associates with Robert Olson Associates, Inc., prepared *The Recovery and Reconstruction Plan of the City of Los Angeles: Evaluation of its Use after the Northridge Earthquake* (NSF Grant No. CMS–9416416), August 1997. The other study is *The Northridge Earthquake: Land Use Planning for Hazard Mitigation* (CMS–9416458), December 1996, by Steven P. French, Arthur C. Nelson, S. Muthukumar, and Maureen M. Holland, all of the City Planning Program at the Georgia Institute of Technology.

county "establish a county-based process for identifying and prioritizing coastal properties so they maybe acquired as part of the state's land acquisition programs." The language has been combined and adapted here in part because it is also possible for the community itself to use state and federal funds to acquire, for example, substantially damaged floodplain properties and to relocate their residents. Tulsa, Oklahoma, and Arnold, Missouri, provide excellent examples of this strategy, in large part because they developed *ongoing* acquisition programs that were already in place before in the predisaster period. (A case study appears in the forthcoming (1998) PAS Report, *Planning for Post-Disaster Recovery and Reconstruction.*) This is, in effect, an "issues and opportunities" component of the natural hazards element.

(e) multiyear financing plan for implementing identified mitigation measures to reduce the vulnerability of buildings, infrastructure, and people to natural hazards that may be incorporated into the local governments operating or capital budget and capital improvement program; and

(f) a plan for managing post-disaster recovery and reconstruction. Such a plan shall provide descriptions that include, but are not limited to, lines of authority, interagency and intergovernmental coordination measures, processes for expedited review, permitting, and inspection of repair and reconstruction of buildings and structures damaged by natural disasters. Reconstruction policies in this plan shall be congruent with mitigation policies in this element and in other elements of the local comprehensive plan as well as the legal, procedural, administrative, and operational components of post-disaster recovery and reconstruction.

(6) The natural hazards element shall contain actions to be incorporated into the long-range program of implementation as required by Section [7–211] below. These actions may include, but shall not be limited to:

(a) amendments or modifications to building codes and land development regulations and floodplain management and/or other special hazard ordinances, including but not limited to natural hazard area overlay districts pursuant to Section [9–101], and development of incentives, in order to reduce or eliminate vulnerability of new and existing buildings, structures, and uses to natural hazards;

(b) implementation of any related mitigation policies and actions that are identified in other elements of the local comprehensive plan;

(c) other capital projects that are intended to reduce or eliminate the risk to the public of natural hazards;

(d) implementation of provisions to carry out policies affecting post-disaster recovery and reconstruction as described in subparagraph (5)(f) above, such as procedures for the inspection of buildings and structures damaged by a natural disaster to determine their habitability as well as procedures for the demolition of buildings and structures posing an imminent danger to public health and safety; and

(e) implementation of provisions to ensure that policies contained in other portions of the local comprehensive plan do not compromise the ability to provide essential emergency response and recovery facilities as described in the local emergency operations program, such as:

  1. adequate evacuation transportation facilities;

  2. emergency shelter facilities; and

  3. provisions for continued operations of public utilities and telecommunications services.

Source: Stuart Meck, Gen. Editor, *Growing Smart*ᔆᴹ Legislative Guidebook: Model Statutes for Planning and the Management of Change, 2002 Edition (Chicago, Ill. American Planning Association, 2002).

Note: Bracketed numbers are references to other sections of the *Guidebook*. Footnote references are from the original text.